How to Become a Sports Official

A Practical Guide to Starting Your Officiating Journey

Mark Bradley
www.artofofficating.com

ISBN-13: 978-1514226995

ISBN-10: 1514226995

Visit www.artofofficiating.com for more information on how to improve as an official.

The information in this book is meant to supplement, not replace, proper officiating training. Like any sport involving speed, equipment, balance and environmental factors, officiating poses some inherent risk. The authors and publisher advise readers to take full responsibility for their safety and know their limits. Before practicing the skills described in this book, be sure your equipment is well maintained, and do not take risks beyond your level of experience, aptitude, training, and comfort level.

Football Icon designed by Freepik from www.flaticon.com

TABLE OF CONTENTS

WHY DOES THIS BOOK EXIST?

The purpose of this book is to help new sports officials navigate through the early process of becoming a sports official. If you are interested in officiating, this book should help answer the "who, what, when, where, why, how" questions you may have. My references and anecdotes will lean primarily towards basketball and football, the sports I officiate in Colorado. "Actual results may vary" in your personal circumstance depending on where you live and the resulting resources you will have at your disposal (although the Internet allows access to multiple valuable officiating forums and websites).

It's crucial for you to be inquisitive and ask as many questions as possible to gain an understanding of your local officiating association and how it works. There is no "one size fits all" approach to officiating, but I believe there are some immutable tenets of officiating that all successful officials embrace. Keep an open mind and set your ego aside as you will initially have a steep - almost vertical - learning curve. As we'll discuss later in the book, if you think you're done learning, you're probably done.

Please contact me through the website below if you have any comments, questions, or input to this book. My passion over the past 30+ years has been teaching and my desire is to offer the most comprehensive new officials guide possible.

Contact Form: www.artofofficiating.com/book-contact

Contact Email: mark@artofofficiating.com

Acknowledgments

I am deeply indebted to multiple men in the Colorado Springs area who have mentored me in my development as an official. A lot of the material in this book has been gleaned from conversations and experiences with these gentlemen.

George Demetriou, a 2014 National Federation of State High School Association's Hall of Fame and 2011 Colorado High School Activities Association Hall of Fame inductee was my instructor in the Colorado Springs Football Officials Association New Officials class and continues to provide valuable mentoring and advice. He is the Colorado football and baseball rules interpreter and has penned multiple articles for Referee Magazine.

Mark VanGampleare, a long-time high school football and high school and college basketball official was my first football crew chief and has provided countless hours of mentoring over meals or by phone/E-mail.

Ray Lutz has officiated more than 2,400 varsity contests, 500 playoff games including 18 state championship football and basketball games, and more than 20 state track and field meets. His "Forward Progress" articles (currently located on artofofficiating.com) are priceless tomes for new and developing officials. Ray was inducted into the Colorado High School Activities Association Hall of Fame in 2004.

Ross MacAskill, now retired, was the referee on my very first football game. Although Ross was a veteran of multiple state championship games, he often volunteered to work the lower-level games with new officials.

DJ Bremser, one of my first instructors, officiates basketball, high school and college football and high school and college girl's lacrosse. I've spent countless hours with DJ on the phone discussing football and lacrosse officiating.

Dennis Wansor officiates high school and college football and boy's/men's lacrosse and high school basketball. Dennis is a student of the game and truly understands the art and science of officiating.

Dave "Crusher" Algood modeled how to be a great football umpire. I worked a ton of games in my first 2 years with Dave in the middle and I would often tell aspiring umpires to observe Dave work a game.

Randy Campbell has officiated basketball and football for 35 years, including 27 years at the Division 1 level in women's basketball and 27 years in college football. He is a PAC-12 Line Judge and has officiated two Conference Championship games, eleven bowl games including the 2013 National Championship Game between Alabama and Notre Dame. As a College Women's Basketball Official, he has worked 25 consecutive NCAA Division 1 Basketball Tournaments (1991-2015), the first WNIT Championship game in 1993, and over 70 conference tournaments. He serves as the Rocky Mountain Athletic Conference Coordinator of Women's Basketball Officials. Randy has been especially helpful in learning how to interact with coaches.

Bill Huffor is an El Paso County Sheriff and is a high school basketball and football official. I've spent quite a bit of time speaking with Bill on the phone or trading texts and Emails.

Andy Heo is an officer in the United States Air Force and currently serves on the Colorado Springs Basketball Officials Association board. Andy and I work in the same building, and we often spend a few minutes to compare notes following basketball games.

There are multiple other officials I could list whom have aided me on my officiating journey. It's important to note the ideas in this Ebook may not completely reflect the officiating philosophies of the men listed above.

FOREWORD BY RANDY CAMPBELL

I was intrigued when Mark told me he planned to write a guide to becoming a sports official. I've spent more than 40 years of my life as a sports official and developing officials is one of my passions. I've officiated Division 1 football for 16 years and Division 1 women's basketball for 27 years, and I'm grateful for the opportunity to be involved in athletics at these levels. In life, a lot of things can be taken away from us - our money, our possessions, our health...but our memories can not be taken away. I had the pleasure and honor to work the 2013 BCS National Championship game between Alabama and Notre Dame, and I'll cherish that memory forever. I've also operated a Colorado basketball officiating camp as Coordinator of Women's Basketball Officials for the Rocky Mountain Athletic Conference that also includes an off-season training program, and I've found helping fellow officials improve their growth and maturation is similarly rewarding.

I started fairly early at the age of 16, officiating softball and baseball in California. As a student at Kansas State University, I needed to make money, so I officiated flag football, basketball, softball, baseball, and even innertube water polo. At the time, minimum wage was $2.35/hour and I found I could make $7.50 working a 1 hour softball game, so officiating made sense financially. As a senior, I officiated the intramural football championship. I loved sports, and I realized I wasn't going to become a professional athlete, so 2 months after graduation from KSU, I started my high school officiating career.

I've read the personal anecdotes in this book, and I agree most veteran officials have made all of the mistakes you'll experience in your first few years. I'll bet my first experience officiating high school football can match anyone's story. I started in a small New Mexico town with 21 officials in our association. We'd meet for 30 minutes or so to talk about officiating and then the veterans would retire to the parking lot to drink beer. On Labor Day weekend, unbeknownst to me, five of the officials decided to go fishing together. One of the association leaders approached me and asked if I'd like to work a varsity game. I had yet to work a single high school game, and he wanted me to start with a varsity game? I assumed he knew I officiated the intramural championships at Kansas

State so I said "of course (gulp), I'd be glad to help out in any way I could." He reached in his briefcase and said, "Here's the mechanics manual; you should probably flip through it." And with my rookie understanding of all things officiating, I looked him in the eye and replied, "I'm not very good with cars." (Thank goodness he thought I was joking!) I looked in the mechanics manual and read something about using a beanbag to mark certain spots. Of course I didn't own a beanbag (I didn't even know it was a part of a football official's gear), so I went to the store, bought a bag of pinto beans and sewed my own beanbag. Luckily, one of the officials on the crew had a spare beanbag, so I was saved the embarrassment of sporting my home-made bag.

When I met with Mark to discuss this book, I asked him "Why do we have officials at sporting events?" This book does a great job unpacking potential motivations for officiating, but it's important to hammer home WHY we have officials. Bottom line, you are on the field or court for two simple but essential reasons: 1) Safety of the players and coaches, and 2) Making sure one team does not gain an advantage over the other team within the rules of the game. It's for these two reasons that rules knowledge and the proper application of rules is such an important concept to understand as you begin officiating. And it's equally important to understand the history behind the rules to understand why specific rules exist. For example, the fourth down fumble rule prohibits anyone but the fumbling player from recovering or advancing the ball during a fourth down play. A single play on September 10, 1978 in a game between the San Diego Chargers and Oakland Raiders was the genesis for this rule. Trailing 20-14, with 10 seconds left, Raiders quarterback Ken Stabler purposefully fumbled the ball forward to avoid a sack. After a swat and a kick, Raiders tight-end Dave Casper fell on the ball in the end zone for the game-tying score. The Raiders received an unfair advantage, and the fourth down fumble rule was implemented the following season. As a San Diego Chargers fan, I still have forlorn memories of this play.

Becoming a good official is like building a house. How do you build a house? You start by building a strong foundation upon which everything else is constructed. The brick walls, beautiful windows and doors, and other features are important, but if you don't spend the time and effort to establish a strong foundation, everything visible above ground will come crashing down around you. It will take discipline and patience to carefully and diligently build a rock-solid foundation that can weather the adversity and challenges you'll face during your officiating career. I've found over the years, people leave officiating for two main reasons: 1) various family issues and 2) their foundation was not strong enough. One of the greatest pieces of advice I can give officials is: worry about things you can control, don't worry about things you can't control. And you definitely have control over how you build your officiating foundation. Reading this book is a positive first step in this process.

This book discusses in great detail the need to find a veteran official to help mentor you through the first few foundational years. This is an essential concept. Have you ever tried to cross a river by navigating over slippery and unsteady rocks and logs? It's best to watch someone who is familiar with the route traverse the obstacles and then exactly follow every step he or she takes. If I don't pay attention, or if I proudly take an alternate, unproven route, I risk dumping in the water. The same applies to following in the footsteps of a mentor. You'll make mistakes, but you'll avoid a considerable amount of frustration if you trust someone to lead you through the rough patches. I've observed too many officials who proudly say, "I'll do it my way!" who unnecessarily fail.

This book also does a great job addressing dealing with coaches. When Mark served as Area Director and Vice President, we collaborated on a briefing titled Dealing with Coaches and Sideline Control. (You can find that information in the Bonus Section.) It's an indisputable fact, officials view the game differently than coaches and have different priorities and goals. Our goal and focus as officials is to safeguard players and to make sure one team does not gain an advantage over the other team within the rules of the game. A coach's goal and focus is winning the game. So, right off the bat, there is a disconnect. We're not approaching the game the same way and we're not talking the same language. That disconnect is the basis for conflict. Accept that by the very nature of the game, there will be numerous instances for the potential of volatile situations to surface. Your continual focus must be to clearly communicate in every scenario. God gave you two ears and one mouth for a reason; the best officials are great listeners.

As you are in the midst of the game, trust your gut and trust your instinct. People that give advice on taking a multiple choice test will tell you to go with your first impression because your first impression is almost always right. See the play and make a decision; don't overthink the call.

In the next section, Mark acknowledges contributions from many talented officials, some of whom have contributed to my officiating career. This book consists of principles and philosophies gleaned from over a hundred years of officiating experience. You've taken a positive step in buying this book as it will help you begin your officiating journey by building a strong officiating foundation.

Chapter 1
How I Started Officiating

One fall Friday night, I went to the local football stadium and begged my way onto the chain crew. I spoke with the Linesman and asked him how I could become involved in officiating. He instructed me to speak with the Referee after the game. I didn't realize that after events conclude, the officiating crew will make a beeline for the locker room. So, I didn't get a chance to speak with the Referee that night. I went home and researched the local football official's association online and sent off an Email query to the point of contact. I contacted the local rules interpreter and asked him to send me a copy of the *Redding Study Guide to NFHS Football Rules*. That summer, I attended my local association's new officials classes and passed the rules exam. After a single scrimmage (where I worked about 20 plays), I officiated my first game at a local junior high school.

I arrived at the school with average rules knowledge (I had twice read the Redding Study Guide cover-to-cover), but I really didn't have an idea of what to call and what to allow at a junior high football game. This was the first game of the season for young players, and I wasn't sure how much "grace" to give. I met in the parking lot with the Referee (a well-respected veteran who had worked multiple high school state championships) and a second year official who would work the opposite wing. I asked the Referee if he could give me some criteria for what to call in the first junior high game of the season. To my dismay, he said, "Let's just work the game and see what happens." The wind was blowing, and the Referee said, "I think we'll see a safety today." On the third play of the game, the Tight End essentially bear-hugged the Defensive End, allowing the Running Back to sweep to my side for about a 25 yard gain. I knew it was a hold, but I didn't know if it was worthy of a flag at the junior high level. So I kept the flag in my pocket. The defensive coach - who happened to be on my sideline - was understandably upset. He hopped up and down on the sideline, waved his arms and yelled, "That's a hold! How could you not see that?" And I thought, "Yes, I did see that blatant hold, and I wish I would have thrown my flag." To my relief, the coach (who later became a very good friend) quickly settled down and we moved on with the game. I also remember throwing two or three flags for illegal formations, which I never should have done in the first junior high school game of the season. The final score was 8-6, and yes, we did have a safety. I guess I did okay...the white hat presented me with a football coin after the game, which I've subsequently passed along to one of my rookie officials after his first game.

After a few years officiating football, I decided to branch out and officiate basketball and girls lacrosse. The process was essentially the same and I soon found myself officiating three high school sports throughout the school year in addition to semi-pro football in the summer.

If you'd like to read more about my personal history, I've included it to the back of the book in Chapter 14 - My History with Sports.

Chapter 2
Motivations for Becoming a Sports Official

My motivation for becoming involved in sports officiating was primarily to be part of the game on the field and court. I didn't start officiating to develop life-long friendships, but I've found over the years I've enjoyed the camaraderie with my fellow officials above all.

There are many motivations for becoming a sports official and you may find more than one of the following applies to you:

- Love of the Sport

- Being a Part of the Game

- Friendship and Camaraderie

- Challenge and Competition

- Physical Fitness

- Supplementing your Income

LOVE OF THE SPORT AND THE ATHLETES

To be an effective official, you need to have a passion for the game. You need to love the sport you are officiating. If you're not passionate about the game or if you don't like being around the athletes, then officiating will quickly become a chore. You'll just be waiting for the game to be over. Being able to enjoy the game is a necessity. As a new official, you'll be working with middle school and high school kids. The game is for the kids, to teach them teamwork, to develop their confidence, to fuel their competitive drive, to help them deal properly with success and failure, to teach sportsmanship, to develop their minds and bodies, and to teach them a life-long passion for sports. If you don't like being around kids and you don't have their best interests in mind, I would highly recommend not becoming an official. You need to enjoy interacting with the kids and have the patience to deal with teenagers, coaches and other officials to become a good official.

BEING A PART OF THE GAME AS AN ARBITER

Sporting events are for the players, the coaches, and the fans. Officials are hired to be impartial arbiters of the contest; as Randy Campbell stated in the Foreword, the reason we have officials is to make sure one team does not gain an advantage over the other team within the rules of the game. Officials should never be the center of attention during the game or insert themselves into the game unnecessarily. However, it is quite a thrill to be part of the contest and to be on the field or court. Running onto the court or field will forever be a thrill for me.

FRIENDSHIP AND CAMARADERIE

The camaraderie and the friendships you will develop are outstanding. You'll be a part of a group of men and women that are like-minded and work together as a team. After the games, many officiating crews may go to a restaurant for a bite to eat to rehash the game. I've found that many of my best friends are guys with whom I officiate. We stay in touch throughout the year and officiate multiple sports together. We attend camps together and hang out in our free time. Don't be surprised if you make meaningful, life-long friendships throughout your officiating career.

CHALLENGE AND COMPETITION

Officiating sports is challenging because you have to be laser-focused on every play to make the right calls; you will need to challenge yourself to study the rules until you know them perfectly. You will challenge yourself to be in the proper position to make the correct call. It's a competition of sorts. You're not competing against the players and coaches. Instead, you're competing to become the best official and the best teammate in the officials organization. If you thrive in situations in which you have to make quick decisions under pressure, you'll love sports officiating.

PHYSICAL FITNESS

Officiating keeps you physically active. As we'll discuss later, you must be in good shape to properly officiate a game. A basketball official will run approximately 3 miles in a game. If you work a double-header (a JV and Varsity game in the same night), you'll need to be physically fit to always be in the proper position to make the proper decisions. Obviously, some sports do not require the officials to run, like volleyball, tennis, baseball, softball, track and field, or swimming and diving. So depending on your passion, you're never "too old" to take up officiating.

My first year of officiating girl's lacrosse was definitely an eye-opener. The girl's lacrosse field is 90-100 yards long from goal to goal, and the playing area behind the goal is another 10-20 yards. With only two officials working most high school games, that's quite a bit of ground to cover. In one particular game, after running multiple consecutive sprints up and down the field, I almost wanted to blow my whistle on a phantom call just to catch my breath! Being able to run up and down a lacrosse field, a football field, or a basketball court definitely requires above-average fitness. I'll discuss physical appearance in more depth later in this book.

SUPPLEMENTING YOUR INCOME

Officiating sports is a great way to supplement your income. There are sporting events played year-round, so if you officiate multiple sports, you can make a significant amount of money. It may not be possible to live off a high school official's game fees but you can make thousands of dollars every year. Your earning potential will vary depending on the state in which you officiate. If you're a college student or individual with a flexible schedule, I would recommend looking into officiating a sport in your local area. You'll make more money than you would at many other jobs. If your schedule is flexible and your afternoons are generally free, you could work a game most every night of the week throughout the year over multiple sports. Unfortunately, a few people are solely interested in making extra money and don't put in any effort to study the rules and get better; my bet is you don't fall into this category as you've purchased this book and have made it this far!

Chapter 3
What Makes a Good Official?

You don't have to fit a specific personality profile to be a good official. There are a lot of excellent officials that aren't very competitive or are fairly quiet and reserved. There are good officials that are outgoing and good officials that are introverted. So, there is no perfect official's personality. However, from my experience, there are some attributes that are common amongst all good officials. If you don't possess many of these characteristics, it may be difficult to be successful and enjoy officiating.

LEADERSHIP

A good official must be a leader. You won't have to lead other officials in your first year or two, but you'll actively lead players and coaches during the conduct of the game. As a leader, you will help shape the game's environment. Your ability to lead and your confidence as an official will be readily apparent to coaches, players, and fans. As you progress in the association, you will be asked to lead a crew and to be the top official at the contest. As the officiating crew's leader, you'll shepherd the crew through the game's phases (preparation, pre-game, game, post-game, and possibly an evaluation). Depending on the sport, you could conceivably stay away from this responsibility (some football officials have worked dozens of years without ever wearing the white hat as referee), but it's not likely. A local soccer referee told me some young soccer officials have quit because they're not willing to move from assistant referee to referee. So bottom line, expect to grow into the role of leader. And oh by the way, you may find yourself leading a crew because there may not be enough seasoned officials to cover all of the games on a given night. So it's a good idea to prepare to lead a crew at the earliest opportunity.

ETHICS

All high school activities associations will have a code of ethics, and you may be required to sign an ethics statement to participate as an official. Codes of Ethics and Codes of Conduct may include consent to issues such as impartiality, recusal from certain games (if you have a connection to an athlete or coach), upholding the game's integrity, abstaining from tobacco products at the game site, preparing physically and mentally (including rules and mechanics study), and agreeing to other stipulations. To be an effective arbiter, you must be a person of high character and ethical conduct. Some state associations may require a background check as part of your eligibility requirements.

JUDGMENT

Good judgment begins with outstanding rules knowledge. If you don't know the rules, you can't make a proper decision about the play that unfolds before you. You also need to understand the "art" of officiating which has multiple aspects: the flow of the game, understanding advantage versus disadvantage - what fouls actually impacted a play's outcome. You will not be an effective official if you insist on a draconian approach to arbitrating the game. Officials will quickly gain a reputation for blowing their whistles too often (calling too many fouls). Randy Campbell states officials are not the "penalty police," and infers there is a balance between "just let 'em play" and blowing the whistle at every indiscretion; it will take practice, study, and discussions with veteran officials to figure out where that line falls. Some sports have "when in doubt" officiating axioms that help officials understand how to adjudicate a specific play. Officials should see the beginning, middle, and end of every play and should not guess about what happened. If you don't see the entire play, you'll have to go with what you've been able to observe.

COMMUNICATION AND RELATIONSHIPS

You obviously need to be able to get along with other people because you're going to be on a crew. It could be a crew of two on a basketball court or a baseball diamond or it could be a crew of five, six, or seven on a football field. As an official, you'll have to get along with members of your crew and you'll have to be able maintain a positive attitude when conflict arises. You should be able to verbally express yourself, especially in stressful environments. But don't worry if you aren't a perfect communicator right now; you'll have multiple years to develop this skill. The better your interpersonal communication skills, the easier it will be to integrate into your local association. Building relationships with other officials can serve you greatly over the years. Networking and nurturing relationships in your local association will aid in your development; you won't progress as a "lone wolf" official. Don't wait to build relationships, start your rookie year and be proactive. Attend every meeting and get yourself on the veterans' radar by actively participating. The veteran officials will notice your enthusiasm and commitment. Another great way to foster relationships is to join or start a rules study group. Distinguish yourself as a hard worker and a potential leader and you will find your opportunities will expand.

BE A STUDENT OF YOUR CRAFT

Additionally, you need to be a lifelong learner. To become a master of the rules and officiating mechanics, it's essential you put in the required study time (there will be a lot of studying!). Don't be satisfied to walk on the field or court with incomplete rules knowledge. How can someone properly officiate a game without complete and accurate knowledge of the rules? You need to be self-motivated, accomplishing the necessary tasks to improve. Don't decide to study only because someone else is requiring it from you or somebody else is motivating you. Desire to be the best rules guy in your group. Bottom line, if you only occasionally open the rulebook, you will not be a successful official. Some plays described in the rule book may happen only once or twice in your officiating career, but you must be prepared to deal with those plays when they occur. Some football officials will simply rely on the Referee or other officials on their crew to know how to enforce fouls. They will approach the game as a follower, and will only throw their flag when "something doesn't look right." They'll report the foul to the referee, but won't have a clue how to enforce the foul. What happens when officials with incomplete rules knowledge are assigned to work a game as the Referee? They'll be in charge without perfect knowledge of the rule book. Or more likely, how do you respond to the coach when he asks for a rule explanation during the pre-game conference or while the game is underway? Rookie football officials start out on the wing, right on the sidelines, and the head coach is within a few feet. Rookie basketball officials are always on the sideline and right in front of the coaches. Poor rules knowledge is the quickest way to lose credibility with coaches and with your fellow officials. Taking the time to open the rulebook on a consistent basis and having good study habits is very important. If you are struggling learning the rules, find a couple of officials - rookies or veterans from your association - and start a rules study group.

You Will Make Mistakes!

As a new official, you are going to make a lot of mistakes. The learning curve for a new official is almost vertical. Like a puppy, you'll have 100% of the energy, but about 20% of the knowledge and situational awareness. Regardless of the number of games you've watched on television, you will always have struggles as you begin your sports officiating career. The game will be ultra-fast, and you'll be hanging on by your fingernails, just trying to keep up. Believe me, after transitioning from fan to official in multiple sports, I can attest the game is so much more than what one sees on television or from the sidelines.

It's not logical to expect a new official to have perfect rules knowledge in his or her first few seasons. So it's inevitable you'll make a rules-related mistake in your first few years. And rules knowledge is only a portion of what you need to know to be a successful official. There is also the mechanics part of the game (where to move to get the best look, how to blow your whistle, where to stand, how to interact with coaches...). So you'll be hanging on for dear life trying to remember the rules, and you'll be hanging on for dear life trying to remember where to stand, when to blow your whistle, and how to report fouls. In your first year or two, you may make a bunch of mistakes every game. Some of the mistakes will be transparent to most coaches, players, and parents. However, unfortunately some mistakes will scream, "HEY, LOOK AT ME!"

I'll never forget my first inadvertent whistle. (Football officials blow their whistle to indicate the ball is dead by rule. So if a football official thinks a live ball is dead and blows the whistle, we call it an "inadvertent whistle".) My mistake was during a first-round playoff game. One team would pooch the kickoff, kicking it high and short to an open area in an attempt to recover the kick. I was the Linesman and was positioned on the 30 yard line. As the ball reached its apex, one of the middle receivers sprinted forward in a mad dash to reach the kick before it hit the ground. As he ran, he waved furiously for a fair catch. I could see a line of players from the kicking team bearing down on the lone receiver with blood in their eyes. There was going to be one heck of a collision if the tacklers didn't hold up. As the ball arrived, I blew my whistle, hoping to protect the receiver from getting blasted. Of course, the receiver muffed the kick, the ball bounded free...and I had blown the play dead! By God's grace, the receiving team recovered the ball. By rule, we had to re-kick the ball. My mistake didn't determine the outcome of the game, but I sure felt bad when we had to line up again for another free kick because of my blunder.

Another mistake that stands out was during a JV game. We only had four officials on that game, so my primary coverage area was a little bigger than with a five-man crew. The team on my sideline fielded a punt, and the runner started towards my sideline. I looked ahead of the runner to observe the wall of blockers. The runner avoided a tackle, was hit, spun, and was hit again, causing a fumble. The kicking team recovered the fumble. The receiving team's coach started to scream at me that his runner's knee was down after the first hit, and that I should have blown the play dead at that moment. Well, even though the runner was about 15 yards away and right in front of me, I failed to look at him during the first contact. The coach chewed my rear end for a good 15 minutes, and there was nothing I could say to appease him. It just so happens I had the same team a few weeks later. The coach recognized me and said, "Hey, I want you to go to our web site, and look at picture #45." When I got home, sure enough, there was a clear picture of me, seemingly looking right at the runner, with his knee clearly on the ground.

The moral of the story is, every veteran official has a big mental filing cabinet full of anecdotes about how he or she screwed up in a game. The key is to have a teachable approach to officiating. YOU WILL MAKE MISTAKES EVERY SINGLE GAME! And you may make the same mistake multiple times in the same season. Always maintain a positive attitude and don't be afraid to receive instruction from other officials; it will only serve to make you better at your craft.

LEARN FROM THE VETERANS

It amazes me when officials react negatively when receiving constructive criticism from other officials. Their defense mechanism after making a mistake is to become self-protective, to rationalize behaviors, and to make excuses. That reaction is basic human nature for many of us; we don't like being called out as inadequate. However, our goal as officials should be to constantly improve, so if someone has a constructive input, we should gladly accept it. It takes a little bit of self-discipline to swallow our pride and listen to others.

Your mistake stories won't be unique. If it happens to you, it's probably also happened to most veteran officials in your association. So, when you are with a veteran and they give you criticism or they bring up areas that need improvement, you need to be able to take that constructive criticism and use it to hone your abilities. They aren't attacking you personally but are genuinely trying to help you improve as an official. Ignore the desire to say "Yeah but," and focus on what your fellow official is trying to say. They are trying to impart some of their hard-earned wisdom to you. Be willing to chuck your pride out the window and absorb their knowledge like a sponge. I recommend keeping a personal journal so you can capture lessons learned from every game you work. It doesn't have to be a play-by-play account of the game. Just record a few short sentences about interesting plays or observations on what you did right and wrong. Your notes will be useful when you start to use film to review your performance. If you have any questions about certain rules, record it in your journal so you can look it up later. The journal will allow you to study the areas in which you need to improve and mark your progress over time. You'll be able to look back in a couple years and see major improvements.

THICK SKIN REQUIRED

You have to begin this endeavor understanding one immutable fact: you will face conflict every single time you step on the field or court. Unless you officiate a friendly competition where the opponents don't care who wins or loses, you'll experience conflict. You shouldn't move to Seattle if you don't like rain and you shouldn't live in Florida if you greatly dislike humidity and bugs. Likewise, you shouldn't become an official if you are conflict averse. You're on the sidelines in close proximity to coaches, players and fans. You also need to understand you're officiating a game with teenagers that haven't fully emotionally matured. The coaches and the fans will definitely have an opinion about how you're doing, especially if you make a controversial call. As a football rookie official working the wings, you'll be right in front of the coaches and if you make a mistake, they're going to let you know about it. So, you need to be thick-skinned and you need to have a sense of humor. You need to be able to take criticism from coaches and fans and not respond out of anger or an inflated ego.

My crew was working a football game between two rivals. The underdog was hanging tough and was down by only seven points. With only a few seconds remaining in the first half, the favored team's quarterback threw a backwards pass to the wideout on the right sideline. The defender properly read the play and closed to make the tackle. The receiver ran toward the middle of the field and juked a couple of tackles. He then ran straight toward the line of scrimmage. Right before he crossed the line, he threw a (legal) forward pass to another player who was standing on the left sideline. That entire portion of the play consumed about 5 or 6 seconds and the scoreboard horn sounded indicating the half had expired. The new ball carrier avoided about three more tackles as he tiptoed down the sideline and dove across the goal line. When I turned to the press box to signal "touchdown," the head coach of the defending team was on the field screaming. I approached him to determine his concern. He yelled the offensive team had linemen illegally downfield. I told the head coach I would check with the Umpire to see if he had noticed linemen illegally downfield. (As I approached the Umpire, I knew whatever happened next would not be good for the officiating crew. Since the broken play had lasted for over 10 seconds, my spider sense was telling me it was likely the linemen had wandered downfield.

23

If we threw a late flag, the head coach of the other team would erupt.)
I approached the Umpire and asked if he had noticed linemen illegally
downfield. When he said he didn't notice linemen illegally downfield, I
knew we were in trouble. The head coach of the team on defense, who
had fought to stay within a single touchdown in the first half, was now
behind by two scores. And he proceeded to spend the next 5 minutes
voicing his displeasure. And we stood there and took it. The entire crew
knew we probably had screwed up the play, and we allowed the coach to
gnaw on us. When we came out to start the second half, I purposefully
stood on that coach's sideline during warmups to allow him to chew on
me some more. The coach was obviously irritated, and we let him voice
his frustration.

THE GAME IS NOT ABOUT YOU!

Fans pay admission to the field or court to watch the athletes play.
They don't pay admission to watch you take center stage during the
contest. The game is not about you! As an official, you are an objective
arbiter, a facilitator, a manager, a liaison, a counselor, a role model.
You exist to ensure the game is played properly within the rules and
that the game flows correctly. Unfortunately, some officials sometimes
approach the game as judge, jury, and executioner. You can quickly
recognize those officials because during pregame or in meetings, they
are the ones who immediately tell tales of confrontations with coaches.
It's almost like they keep a tally of the number of times they whacked a
basketball coach with a technical foul or they threw a flag on a football
coach for unsportsmanlike conduct. Their stories always revolve around
conflict. Good officials know how to resolve conflict without making the
situation "all about them." I've heard some officials say a technical foul
or an unsportsmanlike conduct flag is just a tool in the toolbox, but then
employ that tool at the earliest opportunity. I try my very best to listen
to a coach's concerns and then communicate quietly and carefully why
I made a specific decision. The great majority of the time, a head coach
is satisfied to have that conversation and his or her agitation will be
greatly reduced just because you've spent the time to listen. If an irritated
coach insists on talking over me, I will say "Coach, would you like me
to explain what we saw?" If they don't take the time to listen, I will say,
"I understand your concern coach, and we've discussed this issue. We're
going to move on."

Don't throw your flag on the football field just to make a point. I know of some football crews that will throw a sideline warning flag during the opening kickoff to set the stage for the game. I've also observed officials who quickly assess a technical foul or unsportsmanlike conduct flag to a coach because he or she voices his or her displeasure over a call. In my early officiating years I specifically made it a point to watch veteran officials who were adept at dealing with angry coaches. I paid close attention to how they guided coaches through difficult issues without resorting to the tool of a technical foul or an unsportsmanlike conduct flag. I called them or Emailed them after the game and asked them about the conversations they had with coaches. (I've also found outstanding videos on the internet where officials were mic'd for a game; you'll discover some helpful ways to talk to coaches using that resource.) Officials and coaches are not adversaries on the field. As officials, we need to have the mentality that we are present at the game to facilitate the game. We are not correction officers; we are, in a way, servants. I tell my football crew to operate like employees at a quality restaurant. Be polite, listen and respond, and work your tail off for the customer.

Physical Fitness and Appearance

As stated earlier, to be in the proper position to see a play correctly, you must be physically able to get to the right spot so you can get the best look. You can't be running up the field or court with your tongue hanging out, just trying to keep up with the younger players. The sport you're officiating will dictate the required level of physical fitness and coordination.

The following are examples of sports and the required level of physical effort needed while officiating.

High Intensity: Soccer, Basketball, Lacrosse, Hockey
Medium Intensity: Football
Low Intensity: Baseball/Softball, Tennis, Volleyball, Swimming, Track and Field

Your physical appearance is very important. If you're out of shape and you show up on an athletic field, you'll provide a bad impression to the coaches, players and fans. Also, if you're not physically fit, you'll face a higher risk of injury.

TIME AND AVAILABILITY

Finally, although it is more of a minor characteristic, your availability to work games and attend meetings can determine how well you perform as an official. How much time do you have, especially in the afternoons and the weekends? If you're only able to officiate one game a week, that's fine, and many associations will be glad to have you. However, a first-year official who works four games a week for a single season will typically progress more quickly than a more seasoned official who works one game a week for 2 or 3 seasons. The official who has better availability and works more games will generally learn more and will have a better chance of progressing. Your development as an official is largely based on the amount of experience you have. The more you see, the better you will become. However, it is possible to be a 10+ year veteran and still be a mediocre official. You need to supplement your experience and time spent on the field with rock-solid rules knowledge and good communication skills. As a new official, spend the time to learn the rules. As mentioned earlier, stepping on the field or court with incomplete rules knowledge is a disservice to you, the players, and the coaches. The coaches and players invest an incredible amount of time and effort preparing and practicing for the game you're officiating. A poor call or improper rule enforcement can negate all that hard work.

One of my brothers is an Air Force fighter pilot and graduated from the United States Air Force Weapons School at Nellis Air Force Base in Nevada. The school prepares officers and enlisted airmen to be THE experts in their weapons system. They are the Air Force's version of "Top Gun" graduates. The USAF Weapons School creed is "Humble, Credible, Approachable." Sports officials should embrace a similar creed. Be humble with your attitude towards other officials and coaches and players. The game does not exist for you or to serve you. Be coachable and teachable. Be credible with rules knowledge, physical fitness, and mechanics study. Be approachable and be willing to mentor others and pass your knowledge and skills to others. American entrepreneur Jim Rohn sums up this sentiment with this quote: "The challenge of leadership is to be strong, but not rude; be kind, but not weak; be bold, but not bully; be thoughtful, but not lazy; be humble, but not timid; be proud, but not arrogant; have humor; but without folly."

The opposite of "Humble, Credible, Approachable" is someone who is arrogant, unwilling to accept criticism, and unwilling to learn. Don't be that person. There is a significant difference between being confident and being arrogant. Merriam-Webster defines confidence as "a feeling or belief that you can do something well or succeed at something" and arrogance as "having or showing the insulting attitude of people who believe that they are better, smarter, or more important than other people." It's pretty easy to see the difference between the two attitudes. You MUST have self-confidence to be a successful official. You must walk on the field or the court confident that you will do a great job. But there is a line that goes beyond confident where people become aloof, cavalier, disdainful, and insolent. Be confident, but be humble and teachable. Even long-tenured veterans can learn something new.

One final philosophical question: Should you have played the game to referee the game? In my opinion, it's helpful, but not required. It's helpful as you'll probably have an easier time understanding the rules. If you've played the game, you'll be able to better anticipate player movement and have a better "feel" for the game. However, if you are willing to put in the work to learn the game, you can still be a quality official. After officiating football for 4 years, I decided to become a girl's lacrosse official. I spent multiple hours studying the rules and sitting down with veteran lacrosse officials to learn the game. The US Lacrosse web site was a great tool to develop an understanding of how to officiate the game. Even with all of that preparation, the third time I watched a girl's lacrosse game, I was standing on the field wearing a striped shirt with a whistle in my mouth. Candidly, this wasn't the best situation for the players and coaches, but my partner kept an eye on me and I was able to make it through the game without major issues.

I worked my fanny off learning the rules, studying the mechanics manual, and Emailing and speaking with respected veterans. I made my share of mistakes, but was able to feel more and more confident each game. Despite not playing a single minute of girl's lacrosse, I think I turned into a decent official.

Mark Bradley

Chapter 4
What Makes a Poor Official?

Just as there are characteristics that make good officials, there are definitely some traits that are common amongst poor officials. If you have a bad temper and are easily antagonized into confrontations, if you can't take verbal criticism or have little patience, officiating may not be for you. Are you the kind of person that screams at the television at home or who heckles the officiating crew at a ballgame? If so, officiating is probably not for you. If you don't enjoy working on a team or being around other people, officiating is probably not for you. If you have a huge ego, you feel like you always have to be right, and you always have to defend yourself, officiating is probably not for you. If you complain a lot and you're unable to take criticism, officiating is probably not for you. If you are often late to events, or if you neglect to show up for appointments, you'll definitely struggle as an official. If you're not willing to study, don't take initiative, and if you're not self-motivated, those are probably show-stoppers and probably reasons why you should not consider becoming an official.

Chapter 5

How to Begin

START YOUR OFFICIATING JOURNEY

So how should you start your "journey" to becoming a sports official? With the internet and technology, it's fairly easy. Go to "Google" or another search engine and type in your state and "high school sports association". Your state should have a high school sports and activities association website that will have up-to-date information on your local officials association. I've included a list of links to high school athletics and activities association websites at the end of this book for your convenience. If you can't find information on the internet, call your local high school and ask to speak with the athletic director or his or her secretary. Ask him or her for the name and phone number of the assignor for the specific sport in which you are interested. Be proactive and call the points of contact you can find. Email them and persist in your efforts to contact them until you receive a reply. There's no telling how responsive your association's point of contact will be. If you Email or call and you don't hear anything back, keep trying. Many times in the off season, the point of contact may be officiating another sport or may not view connecting with new recruits as a top priority.

Youth/Rec League Sports

You can also officiate Youth or Rec league sports. The players will be younger and the skill level will be lower but if you want to start with a slower pace, this would be the level of officiating for you. Just note, parents may give you more grief at the Youth/Rec league level than at the Junior High or High School level. Depending on your area, you may not receive the same level of training and support that a high school association would provide.

Start Early with Self-Study

After you research your local association and find a good point of contact, you need to remain proactive. You can even start your own self-study in the off-season. Ask your new point of contact for a rules book or a study guide. There are many resources to help you get started. If you're able to get your hands on some study materials, start studying right away. Don't wait for the first formal class. Online forums like www.refstripes.com, www.artofofficiating.com and www.davehallofficiating.com are valuable resources for football and basketball. If you're officiating a different sport, Google "your sport" + "officiating forum" to find helpful online resources (Youtube is full of instructional videos). George Demetriou's Redding Study Guide to NFHS Football is a great tool. In fact, I highly recommend the Redding Study Guide as the first purchase for any new football official. If you're looking for a resource with up-to-date information and articles written by veteran officials all over the country, Referee Magazine might be what you need. As the season approaches, your point of contact will be able to give you information about rookie classes and other rookie training. Some associations may run classes during the week in the off-season to help new officials learn the rules and mechanics. Some offer classes two or three times a week for two to three months. Some smaller associations may only meet a couple of times during the season. And unfortunately, you may run into a situation where you are pretty much on your own in learning how to officiate the sport you selected. So it is important that you are able to study on your own if needed.

A fellow official told me a story about when he first started football officiating. He went to the first meeting expecting rules study and rookie training. Instead, someone pointed to him and asked, "Are you able to work this game? Good, you're on the crew." As he and two other guys were driving together to the game, they were trying to determine who would be the referee; no one readily volunteered because they were all rookies or relatively new officials. In the car on the way to the game, they were furiously flipping through the rule book trying to learn as much as they could. They threw only one flag the whole game because they didn't know how to enforce fouls.

I hope that experience won't happen to you, but be prepared to "fill in the gaps" on your own. The more prepared you are for the unexpected, the more confidence you'll have in calling a good game.

WILL OR SKILL

I believe everything in life is either a "will" issue or a "skill" issue. As a brand new official, you'll have low "skill" (you won't know the rules and the mechanics required to be an effective arbiter). However, as a brand new official, you'll (hopefully) have high "will" (you'll be excited about learning). Over time, your skill will definitely improve and (hopefully) you'll retain your enthusiasm and work ethic. Unfortunately, there are veteran officials who have been around for a while, but who are still "rookie" officials in knowledge and competence. They are described as being "First-Year officials 20 years in a row." Because of a "will" issue or a "skill" issue, they don't seem to grow. Other officials will have high skill (they know the rules and understand how to officiate the game) but are difficult to be around. Much of your growth will be in your direct control; if you want to be an effective official, you'll need to maintain your enthusiasm and desire (will) to learn and improve (skill) throughout your officiating career.

THE START OF FORMAL TRAINING

When you go to your first training class, you should expect to focus on the rules. They won't teach you about mechanics, where to stand on the court/field, how to blow your whistle, or how to talk to coaches. Instead, you will learn the "science" of officiating...the rules. Plan on attending every meeting because you want to develop a strong foundation. It's like taking a high school or college course; if you skip or miss a class, you're missing an important lesson which will potentially create a gap in your knowledge foundation. If you miss a meeting, you may be able to sit down one-on-one with the instructor and spend some time on the lesson. Taking them out for lunch or dinner is usually enough of a bribe to get them to spend an hour or 2 talking about what you missed. You need to commit to self-study. If you enjoy learning, it won't be hard. However, if it has been multiple years since you were in high school or college, it might be a little more difficult. You need to discipline yourself to carve out a couple of minutes or hours every day to dive into the rules and other resources. Also, the formal classes will not be able to cover everything that's in the rulebook because there just isn't enough time. You'll have to supplement the classroom teaching with a lot of self-study. Before my rookie football season, I read the entire Redding Study Guide twice, cover-to-cover to prepare for the rules exam. You may think that you understand the rules because you've watched games on TV, you're a parent of a player, or you played in high school or college, but you must understand the rules are orders of magnitude more complex than what you think you know. NFL rules, college rules and high school rules are significantly different, so you may need to re-learn or unlearn rules you think you know. I will often be heckled from the stands because a parent or fan saw a rule interpretation from a college game on Saturday or an NFL game on Sunday and expected the high school rule to be the same.

THE LEARNING CURVE

Expect a steep learning curve. It's like learning a new language. There will be plenty of acronyms and rules with which you are not familiar. Don't be surprised if you are overwhelmed at first. You may feel like you are quickly falling behind, but know that everyone started as a rookie. Most likely, even the most seasoned officials in your association had the same struggles you did. (For fun, ask some of the veteran officials about personal anecdotes from their earliest years.) If you stick with it and show a positive attitude, there will be veteran officials who will notice your enthusiasm and will be happy to spend additional time with you. Strive to make it over the learning hump and you'll find all your hard work will pay off. Bottom line: You MUST be a rules expert. Don't give yourself permission as a first year official to be lax in your rules knowledge. A coach can ask you any question about the rules and you need to be able to respond with authority and confidence. Not knowing the rules will destroy your credibility with coaches. Strive to know the rules better than any other official in your association.

HOW TO STUDY THE RULES

There many different ways to learn the rules. There are multiple web sites that dissect learning styles; I've discovered the major styles of learning are Visual (Images and Pictures, including Video), Auditory (Listening), Read/Write (Good old-fashioned reading!), and Kinesthetic (Acting out and using physical objects). You probably also prefer to study alone (Solitary) or in a group (Social). Figure out what works best for you, and then stick with that method. For example, if you are an auditory learner, you'll probably want to get into a study group so you can hear someone else talk about the rules. When I was an instructor at the Air Force Academy, I heard of a cadet who chose to re-enact military conflicts so he could remember details to prepare for an exam.

When I read my rulebook every year, I take a highlighter and highlight all the rules that I need to review or refresh in my mind. Some of the more obscure rules that will rarely happen during a game situation are often the rules that need to be reviewed. My highlights will then remind me where I need to spend a little extra time. As you study the rules, keep notes in the margins with a pencil. Marking up your rulebook will help you internalize the information. You can even use the notes you write to help review the rules with your mentor. If you're confused about a rule, jot it down and ask questions in your next new officials class or when you meet with your mentor. You can also go online and post a question on an officiating forum.

Flashcards are helpful with rules and enforcement of penalties. Break out the 3"x5" notecards and build a flashcard deck for the rules with which you are struggling. If you don't want to spend the time making physical flashcards, download a flash card app and make some digital ones.

You can find reviews of the top rated Flashcard Apps at www. artofofficiating.com/flashcards

Some associations will provide casebooks that provide situational plays and scenarios described in detail that help you learn the rules and how to enforce them.

As a rookie official (and as a veteran official), your knowledge of the rules is crucial to your success. As discussed earlier, if you find it difficult to dive into the rule book and absorb the rules and concepts alone, you might want to find or form a study group. Study groups are a great way to dig into the more complex concepts because of the variety of perspectives each official will bring to the table. Adding the social element of a study group can break through the banality of learning the rules and can help to form some great friendships. If your association doesn't offer a formal rules study group, grab a few of the rookie officials and start your own. If you're not comfortable running the group yourself, find a veteran official with a solid rules foundation and ask him/her to help mediate. From week to week, there may be a particular rule or topic to study. Volunteer to teach one of those sessions. It is amazing how much you are able to learn when you are responsible for teaching something to another person. Let's be practical, the rules aren't "sexy" and can get boring at times. Remember, the learning curve for officiating in most sports is nearly vertical, and you'll discover concepts and rules that you didn't realize existed. The rules can be very complex and it's important that you learn them properly. A veteran with excellent rules knowledge can keep your study group on the straight and narrow.

TEST TIME

Typically, at the end of the rookie classes, there will be a rules test. The test may be a closed book paper test or an open book online test. The passing score/percentage is different depending on the association and/or state. Depending on your score, there may be different levels of officiating for which you will be qualified or certified. You could be a provisional official or an apprentice official or an official with full "rights." If you didn't do well the first time, you may be given the opportunity to retake the test immediately or later in the season. You may think that passing the rules test is a breeze, but as a new official with little rules experience, the test can be very challenging. Don't expect to pass if you only cram for a couple hours the night before. Hit the books and study often and you should be able to pass the test on your first try.

Chapter 6
After the Test

CREW VS POOL

There are multiple arrangements for organizing officials in an association. Some states use a crew concept where a fixed crew will work the season's games together. Others employ a pool concept where assignors select officials for individual games based on objective or subjective criteria. Some organizations assign ratings to separate officials into levels which helps with scheduling. The rating of an official can change year to year based on ability, experience and subjective analysis. If your association uses ratings to classify officials, it is important to understand the criteria that is used to grade officials. With a firm grasp of the criteria, you will be able to set specific goals. For example, your association may highly encourage attendance at a camp during the off-season. Regardless of the organization method used, your enthusiasm, rules knowledge, comportment, reliability, judgment and physical fitness are all factors the association leadership will consider when making crew draft or rating decisions.

After you've passed the test, depending on what state you are officiating in and what sport you are officiating, you will be assigned to a crew or you will be part of a "pool" as an independent contractor. As a rookie official you can expect to be working junior high and sub-varsity games/matches. You won't be working varsity games right away regardless of your test score. There may be a few exceptions - my first girl's lacrosse game (and the third game I had ever observed) was a high school varsity game. Many swimming leagues do not have JV programs, so your first swimming meet could very well be at the varsity level.

A quick word on working sub-varsity or lower-level varsity games. Regardless of your assigned game, you should give the players and coaches your best effort. The seventh grade basketball player, the #5 singles tennis player, the freshman football player, or the JV volleyball player experiences the same level of excitement and pre-game jitters as the big-time varsity athlete. Work as hard at the junior high intramural game as you would a 5A varsity game. The coaches will recognize and appreciate your high level of effort and interest.

Many football associations use a crew system. The exact makeup of the crew will differ according to association and/or state. Some crews consist of five people that work every game together. Other crews are much larger (10-15 officials) which provide the manpower for officiating all the different levels of junior high and high school football (Freshman, JV, Varsity). Some associations assign games at the state level while other associations have multiple assignors for different leagues in the same city. If you're drafted onto a crew, provide as much information as possible to the crew chiefs. You should include your experience (if you have officiated any other sports) and when you are available to officiate. Good availability is a major factor for crew chiefs and assignors when you are being drafted to a crew or assigned a schedule. Being available early in the day is major benefit because the majority of the sub-varsity games are played in the early afternoon during the week or early in the morning on weekends.

YOUR ORGANIZATION AND ITS STRUCTURE

The organization and structure of your local association can vary widely according to state, sport, and city. A typical hierarchy could include a city/region sport association subordinate to a state sport association subordinate to a state high school activities association. There may also be a national sport association. In some cases the national organization may have authority over state sport organizations or it may only provide rules and safety training. Let's use Colorado high school football as an example. There are local associations like Denver (DFOA), Colorado Springs (CSFOA), and Pueblo (PFOA), that are under the Colorado Football Officials Association (CFOA). The Colorado High School Activites Association (CHSAA) in Denver is the governing body for all high school activities in Colorado and is above both the CFOA and CSFOA. The National Federation of State High School Associations (NFHS) provides safety guidelines, rules, training materials, and leadership to state high school activities associations.

Depending on how your organization is set up, you could pay local association, state, and possibly national association dues. The dues pay for governing infrastructure, meeting location rental, insurance for you as an official, post-season awards, and other services your association might use.

The leadership of your organization will also vary. It typically consists of a board made up of members of the association elected by the membership. Crew chiefs, board members, and potentially even the game assignor hold most of the local decision-making authority. Associations typically have an assigned or elected "Rules Interpreter" who is the rules guru. (There is usually a state rules interpreter for each sport and a local rules interpreter for each local city/region association.) His/Her job is to communicate rule changes and provide insight into rules interpretations to leadership/members of the association. The state interpreter attends annual national conferences to discuss and vote on rule changes. It is the job of the local association to provide training, structure, and possibly game assignments. State associations govern the local associations and provide policy and leadership. As a rookie, focus on your local association and leadership.

BEGINNING POSITIONS

In football, you'll start on the wing as a linesman or line judge. You probably won't be a referee during your first couple of seasons but you should strive to get there as quickly as possible. (I purchased a white hat during my first year of football to set a goal for advancement.) You may work the middle of the field as an umpire fairly quickly. (If you've never worked as an umpire, find a veteran umpire that you respect and pick his/her brain over a meal.) Swimming officials may only rule on turns and strokes until they are more familiar with the rules and how to arbitrate a swim meet as an official. Soccer officials will work the lines as assistant referees. In basketball, baseball, and lacrosse, you may begin with 2-person mechanics. Most states will use 3-person mechanics at the varsity level; you'll eventually get there. As you learn, go to a varsity game and specifically watch the positions you'll work at the sub-varsity level. Watch how the officials move to get a better look. Watch how they communicate with coaches, players, and with each other. In football, you'll eventually gravitate toward positions you enjoy. (Some really enjoy working in the middle as an umpire. Others like working in front of coaches as a wing.) If your association is short on umpires and/or back judges, you may decide to specialize in those positions after your first few years to advance more quickly. I highly recommend you don't focus on a few specific positions in your first few years as this will limit your growth opportunities. Also, don't be afraid to work into a football white hat (Referee) position. This will force you to study the rules a little harder (as you will be ultimately responsible for penalty enforcement) and will also allow you to see the field with a different perspective.

How Scheduling Works

Most large associations use an automated assignment system like Arbitersports.com to manage their schedules. Smaller associations may just use an excel spreadsheet, the phone, and Email to communicate with their officials. There is a good chance you'll be using an automated assignment system. Your assignor should explain how the system works and will talk you through how to register and add contact information. A few words of advice: The assignor will ask you to block the days and/or times you can't work. So if you work until 4:00pm, ensure you block until about 5:00pm, depending on how far you work or live from contest sites. If you don't appropriately block dates and times, you'll have to decline assigned games. If you decline too many games, the assignor may begin to offer games to others. It wouldn't hurt to send an Email to the assignor with specific information (i.e., "I normally work until 3:00pm, but if I get at least a week notice, I can coordinate with my boss to get off work early"). The assignor will assign a game to you or your crew and you'll receive an Email notification from the assignment system saying you have been assigned new games. You can then log in to the website and accept or decline the game according to your schedule. All the information you'll need including the location, time, and other officials assigned to the game will be made available online. Some assignors will schedule the entire season at once and some will schedule a month at a time. As previously stated, you should expect lower level games for the first couple of years. However, always be prepared to officiate at the next level. Be prepared to work a game at a different position. Your hard work and initiative will help you progress quickly.

If your association uses an automated assignment system (like Arbiter), you will be able to view the master schedule with available slots. Ask whomever does the assigning if he/she would mind if you contact him/her to indicate your availability for open slots for a game. But, let me be clear - some assignors don't want a bunch of "back seat drivers" with the schedule. It's most likely the assignor already has officials selected for the open positions. However, it doesn't hurt to check if the assignor doesn't mind the query.

FIND A MENTOR

In my opinion, the following paragraph is one of the most significant parts in this book! Find a mentor as soon as you can to help you develop more quickly. Keep your eyes and ears open for officials others in your association respect. You can even ask other officials for their recommendation of who would make a good mentor. Introduce yourself to veteran officials and spend time with them. If you like the way your personalities mesh and you respect and trust them as an official, ask them to be your mentor. Let them see your enthusiasm and effort. Your mentor doesn't have to be an official that's been working for 30 years. You can find driven, respected officials that have five or six years of experience who would enjoy helping you develop. Having a mentor is very important in your development as an official. Ask your mentor to come to a couple of your games and critique your performance. Your mentor can quickly identify your strengths and weaknesses and make suggestions about what you need to improve. Don't just rely on your game partner(s) to provide feedback; they will be focused on their primary coverage areas and won't be able to closely watch you. They also won't be able to take detailed notes during the game. If your mentor is unable to attend a game or two, request video footage from the schools and send it to your mentor for feedback. If your mentor can't attend, ask a couple of other veteran officials to watch you officiate and have them provide very specific criticism. If your association uses an automated assignment system like Arbiter to assign games, you can look at the master schedule and determine if a veteran official you respect is working the game after your game. Then you can contact the official to see if he or she can come a little early to watch your game and provide feedback. After you work a game, call or Email your mentor or the person who watched you work and discuss plays or situations.

> *In my first year of basketball officiating, I experienced a play at the end of the game in which a team was out of timeouts and down by four points with about 7 seconds to play. The team that was behind scored a two point field goal, and as the ball fell through the basket and hit the floor, one of the players slapped the ball away so his teammates could set up to defend the inbounds pass. I blew my whistle and reported a delay of game warning to the table. Later, when I discussed this play with my mentor, he asked me, "Did the player who slapped the ball away gain an advantage for his team, or did he actually make the situation worse? Could you have simply allowed the clock to run while the other team collected the ball?"*

By discussing this play with someone I respected, I was able to learn a valuable lesson. In the same light, if you've had a difficult conversation with a coach, or if you've "butted heads" with a fellow official, ask your mentor how you could have better dealt with the situation.

TRANSITION FROM RULES TO MECHANICS

You've passed the test and you're a rules expert. Now it's time to work on the "art" of officiating, the mechanics and comportment with coaches and players.

- Where do you stand?

- How do you move on the field to improve your look at the play?

- How do you blow your whistle?

- How do you throw your flag as a football official?

- How do you report fouls to the table as a basketball official?

- How do you talk to coaches?

- What do you do during pre-game?

Randy Campbell says officiating is really easy, with the exception of one problem...players move. Even the best officials cannot see through players' bodies, so officials must move to get the best look to see between players. A huge part of mechanics training is learning how to get that best look.

In some sports such as soccer and swimming/diving, the rule book may be thinner, but that doesn't mean your job will be easier. The United States Soccer Federation (USSF) Laws of the Game (rule book) are actually pretty short - only about 50 pages. However, there are companion documents (Advice to Referees) that go into greater depth about the "intent' behind the Laws of the Game. Because of the fluid nature of soccer, the "intent" of the rules are important. There are many fouls that go "recognized but uncalled" because the attacking team maintained the momentum of the attack (advantage). Lacrosse is similar as the official must acknowledge "I saw that foul," but will allow a player to continue the attack. Advantage/disadvantage is a concept that will be discussed in sports such as soccer, football, hockey, basketball, and lacrosse. This is the "art" of officiating.

As you make the transition from rules knowledge to mechanics knowledge, I recommend you spend some one-on-one time with your mentor and talk about mechanics. Hopefully, your association has a mechanics day after your test. If they don't, ask for one. When I began officiating girl's lacrosse, I worked portions of two games at a "play day" (scrimmage). My next time on the field, I worked a varsity girl's game. So, depending on your association, you may get thrown into the deep end of the pool to learn how to swim. Don't panic, just do the best job you can and work your tail off. Be proactive in learning your mechanics. You can watch games on TV or on the internet. Believe me, when you start officiating, you'll never watch a game on TV the same way again. Instead of watching the players, you'll find yourself observing the officials! While there is a certain level of on-the-job training involved with officiating, you should be as prepared as possible when you arrive for your first game. Don't show up at your first game wishing you could have better prepared. You want to be proud of the amount of effort you've put into learning the rules and mechanics.

Learn from Your Mistakes

Nelson Bosell stated, "The difference between greatness and mediocrity is often how an individual views a mistake." As discussed earlier, it's important to acknowledge as a developing official, the mistakes you make are never unique. Other officials have made every single mistake you will make. Do not obsess or grieve over a mistake; learn from it and move on. Your focus needs to be on the play at hand and not on a play that happened 5 minutes ago. Don't get defensive when another official approaches you with constructive criticism. The worst thing to say is "yeah but" because you're defensive or not open to developing your technique or mechanics. Not everything you hear will be perfect advice; write the criticisms down in your journal and share them with your mentor or other veterans. There is no such thing as a perfect game. No official has worked a game free of mistakes. Mistakes and loss of focus will happen, so give yourself permission to fail but strive for excellence.

Emulate Respected Veterans

Another great way to learn is by watching other officials. As discussed earlier, if your association uses Arbiter to schedule games, you can find the master schedule and determine if there are officials working a game following your game. Try to stay for at least half of the game. As the old saying goes, "values and attitudes are caught, not taught." Similarly, you can "catch" a lot by watching other officials work. Attend games that your mentor or other officials you respect are working and look at how they handle themselves, how they speak with the coaches, and the details of their mechanics. As a first year football official, I remember observing the emotional response of a wing official after he collided with a coach on the sideline. Instead of losing his temper, he calmly threw his flag, calmly reported the foul to the Referee, and then calmly interacted with the coach. I will never forget how he maintained his composure during the entire time. He didn't get angry at the coach, even though I'm sure the blind-side collision probably shook him a little.

Keep detailed notes of everything you observe that you can later review. Ask permission to sit in on pregames and see how other officials prepare for games. Be a sponge and absorb all the knowledge you can. Referees of varsity football games are very open to letting first year officials sit in on pregames and will often let you work on the chain crew or walk the sidelines with their wing officials. If you're able to sit in on pregames, be a fly on the wall. A crew preparing for a game doesn't need a rookie interrupting or asking questions. Write down any questions you have and save them for your mentor. Observe how the officials discuss plays at halftime and how they resolve differences of opinion.

Chapter 7
Equipment and Physical Appearance

How You Should Look

If we're completely candid with ourselves, we know if our physical appearance is acceptable. But if you have any doubt, watch a college football or basketball game on TV and note the professional appearance of the officials; that should be your standard. College and NFL officials are typically in great shape. Use them as a template, but ask your local association what their guidelines are for physical appearance and fitness. Some associations will not allow overweight officials to work televised games. You won't work a TV game as a brand-new official, but you should always strive to exceed standards.

Your Hair and Clothes

What is your association's policy on facial hair and hair length? Do they prohibit or discourage facial hair? I guarantee you will not see a single college or professional official with a beard, and very few wear mustaches. Their hair will be cut relatively short. It's just not deemed professional to have a "shaggy" look. If you go to an off-season camp overweight or sporting facial hair, you'll receive a comment about it. If you decide to have facial hair, it should be well groomed and neat. You should never officiate with a 1 or 2 day growth. What do you wear when you arrive at the facility? I've read it takes only 7 seconds to make a first impression, so even if you're "just passing by" on the way to the dressing room, a coach will develop an opinion about you based on what you are wearing. Shorts and a sweatshirt will tell a different "story" than business casual. In my opinion, what you wear to/from the game will reflect the amount of respect you have for the game and for the coaches and players. I've even received advice from veteran officials that your "uniform" includes your vehicle. If you show up in a filthy vehicle, that will undoubtedly serve as a poor first impression. So some officials ensure their cars are clean before they arrive at a facility. Your car doesn't need to be new, just clean. Everything about your appearance, including the cleanliness of the vehicle you drive into the parking lot, impacts first impressions.

UNIFORM APPEARANCE

Your uniform is part of your appearance. What does the word "uniform" mean? Dictionary.com defines "uniform" as "identical, constant, or without variations in detail." It implies that all the officials on the field will look the same; same hat, same shoes, same color football bean bags. You don't want to stand out because your uniform looks different than all the rest. Crews that are dressed the same look more professional and look better in general. Most associations want fitted hats, not hats with adjustable backs. You don't want to wear an adjustable cap when everyone else is sporting a fitted hat. If you stand out for the wrong reasons, you'll draw unwanted attention and will give coaches and parents one more thing to point out. How about shoe color? Are your field shoes all black or are white stripes allowed? Also, you want to make sure your uniform items are serviceable which means they're not worn out, they're clean and well-pressed. You want your shoes to be shiny. This will help you look professional at all times. Check with your crew leader or association about where you should change into your uniform. For football, varsity crews typically change at the school or stadium in a locker room. For sub-varsity football games, you typically won't have access to changing facilities, so you'll most likely arrive to the game dressed. For basketball, you'll almost always dress in the school. The rule of thumb is always look your best for the public. Don't show up at the game half-dressed in your officiating uniform. It gives the wrong first impression. You want to either show up completely dressed in your officiating uniform or dressed in acceptable clothing (think business casual). Your association may have guidelines regarding this issue so make sure you comply with their direction. Does your association prohibit jeans or shorts? Find out and then comply with their expectations.

Bottom line: You're in control of the "first impression" you convey to players, coaches, and fans. The way you look, the way that you carry yourself, as as mentioned earlier, even the cleanliness of your car gives an impression.

Acquiring Your Uniform

Uniform items are typically purchased online. Some larger cities might have a uniform distributor or a local store that sells officiating uniforms. Most of the time, your uniform items will be purchased online from retailers such as **Honig's, Cliff Keen, Purchase Officials, Smitty Official's Apparel, or Coaches Choice**. Make sure you check with your association and get very clear expectations and directions as to what you should buy. For example, most uniforms have an American flag. Does the flag have a gold border or a white border? What color are the football bean bags (white, blue, or black)? All these little details are important. Your mentor can help you immensely with this step of the process. They know exactly what you need and may even be able to loan you some equipment. Ask about sunglasses, pants, flags, etc. Don't make any purchases without confirming what's expected with the association. When I was a brand new official, I purchased the incorrect flags online. I bought cloth flags with a weight sewn into the middle. They looked really nice, but I could only throw that type about 10 yards. I had to go back on the website and order the correct flags, the "long toss" flags made of nylon. This cost me both time and money. In some cases, your association may have uniforms and/or equipment on hand for rookies.

Equipment Bags

Depending on the sport you are officiating, you'll need a black equipment bag to hold all your gear. Sports like football require a large bag. I bought a High Sierra bag for football 4 years ago and I absolutely love it. For basketball you'll need a small to medium size suitcase or gym bag. If it gets cold during the season for a sport played outdoors, you'll need an even larger bag to hold all your cold weather gear. For girl's lacrosse, I used a black back pack. I highly recommend purchasing a bag with rollers because you'll be lugging this bag in and out of cars and locker rooms. Make sure you buy a quality bag that will last. It will take a lot of punishment over the season so it's worth spending a little more money on something that will last more than one season.

For football officiating, each bag will probably need to hold the following uniform items and equipment:

- Long Sleeve Shirt

- Short Sleeve Shirt

- Shorts

- Long Pants

- Jacket

- Field shoes

- Hats

- Underarmour Gear

- Smaller bag or other container for belt, flags, bean bags, whistles, coins, etc

- Towel

- Shampoo, soap, deodorant

- Combination Lock

The items you'll need to store in your bag will vary according to climate/weather and the sport you are officiating. For instance, football requires much more gear than lacrosse or basketball.

A lock is important when you're changing in a locker room or coach's office. If there are lockers at the location, make sure you secure your valuables in a safe location. Some officials choose to leave wallets and cell phones in their cars. As always, talk to your mentor and/or association to see what they recommend.

Chapter 8
Money and Travel

TRANSPORTATION AND TRAVEL

You'll be doing a lot of driving to and from games so a reliable form of transportation is required. Most of the time you'll be traveling by yourself to games in your local area. If you're on a crew that is officiating a game out of town, you'll typically meet at a centralized location and carpool together as a crew. It's very important to be at the meeting location ahead of the scheduled time and with all your gear ready to go. The Referee or the official that is in charge of the crew will typically be the driver and receive any mileage reimbursement in addition to their game fee. Depending on where you live, you may travel to a town that doesn't have a convenience store close to the school, so you may want to bring some snacks and drinks for after the game. Depending on the sport and your association, you may sometimes be asked to work a game 3+ hours away because there are no nearby officials. However, for most officials, the majority of assigned games will be local. If you do have to travel a long distance to work a game, have fun with your crew on the road trip. You'll be surprised how much you learn.

BE PREPARED

Some crew chiefs will decide on the uniform combination at the game site so make sure you bring everything you could possibly need. The weather in many states (like Colorado!) can change drastically in a few short hours so it's better to be prepared for all uniform combinations. You don't want to be the odd one out who failed to bring a long-sleeved shirt when it gets cold outside. Before you leave for the game or for work that morning, double and triple check your gear. You could be traveling 50+ miles away and won't be able to run home and grab something you forgot. If it helps, make a checklist and go down the list checking off every item. I would even recommend having two of everything. Equipment will break or wear out and your crew partners may forget something. Having a backup is important, especially when traveling out of town. Before my first game I checked my bag five or six times. I knew in my head that I had everything but I still wanted to make sure I didn't leave an item out of my bag. Even as a veteran official, I've left shoes and pants at home. When you work multiple games during the week, sometimes you lose track of what is in your bag and what is in the laundry. Getting ready for the game is like preparing for an important written test. You want to make sure you get lots of rest. You never know if the schools will provide refreshments for halftime. Toss a couple of granola bars and bottles of water or gatorade in your bag just in case.

INITIAL COST AND MAINTENANCE

There is a financial cost to get started but, depending on the sport, you should be able to recoup your initial investment with a couple of game checks. The three main costs when you start are dues, study materials, and uniforms/equipment. There are dues that you'll have to pay every year to both your local association and your state and/or national organization.

The sport will dictate how much equipment/gear you must acquire. Some associations provide uniforms for rookies to defray the initial cost, but most require you to make the uniform purchases. Before purchasing uniforms and equipment, make sure you are getting exactly what you need. Just because an item is for sale on a web site doesn't mean it's the proper item for your state, association, or crew (for example, some crews will use only a certain bean bag color). Talk with your mentor or a veteran official before you make a major purchase. Don't go to the local sporting goods store and buy the first striped shirt you see. It's probably the wrong one. If you live in a region of the country where it gets cold, you may need to buy additional cold weather gear which can be fairly expensive..

- Local dues ($20-30)

- State or national dues ($80-$85)

- Study guides and training materials ($15-$30)

- Uniform items (Depends on sport and weather)

The first year is the most taxing financially. In your first year, only buy essential items. Each subsequent year, you'll most likely purchase additional optional equipment (such as a timing device for the football play clock). You'll also get great ideas for equipment by observing what other officials use. (After one game, I came home and "stole" one of my wife's tupperware containers because it was perfect for storing smaller football officiating items such as cards, whistles, pencils, flags, bean bags, etc.) You may also see a particular bag you like or a device to keep your uniform items from becoming wrinkled. Once you have the uniform items, it's just a matter of maintenance and replacing items that are no longer serviceable. Don't ever wear a uniform item that is worn, frayed, or discolored. Remember, your personal appearance is very important and if you wear worn out gear, it will reflect poorly on you. Depending on the sport you're officiating, you'll be putting a lot of miles on your shoes so make sure to budget for at least one new pair of shoes every season or two.

Keep track of the uniform items you purchase for officiating as you'll be able to deduct those expenses when you file your taxes.

HOW YOU GET PAID

You'll get paid by the schools in multiple ways. Some schools will pay you in cash. Other schools will collect your personal information on site and will send you a check. Many other schools will use a web site such as Refpay.com to pay you electronically. When you join your association, you'll most likely register with an automated assignment system like Arbitersports.com and with Refpay.com. On Refpay, you'll provide financial information (bank routing and account numbers). After you work a game, you'll typically see funds from the school added to your Refpay account within about a week. I recommend you keep a spreadsheet of your games so you can keep track of payments. If you think you're missing a payment, Email your crewmates and see if they've received payment. If you are sure you did not get paid for a game, contact the athletic secretary at the school to see if the school submitted payment. If you run into a problem you can't resolve, speak with the assignor and see if he or she can provide any help or advice.

You are an independent contractor, so you'll also need to keep track of your income for tax purposes. If you make enough money with a specific school district, you'll receive a Form 1099-MISC with the total amount you earned from that source.

TIME COMMITMENT

Your time commitment will vary according to the sport you officiate. Officiating a football game will take more time than a lacrosse or basketball game and typically requires a larger time commitment. If you consider how much time is spent preparing and officiating a game and compare it to how much money you are making, you aren't making a lot at the high school level. You can spend five hours or more officiating one football game including drive time and pregame. Those five hours may make you fifty or sixty dollars. Again, the amount of money you make will vary by state and level of competition. You probably won't make a living officiating at the high school level, but it can greatly supplement your income, especially if you officiate multiple sports throughout the year.

I know this is getting into your personal business, but I want to comment quickly on how this significant time commitment may impact your family. Many associations hold weekly meetings during the season and if you work three or four games each week, you'll be gone most evenings during the season. Make sure you discuss this with your family so they have clear expectations. Also, ensure you speak with your boss about having to leave work early on some days. It can become a balancing act (officiating, family, and work) and you don't want to finish the season with hard feelings.

Chapter 9

Game Day

THE PREGAME

Before you show up at the location, make sure you have communicated with the crew chief or whomever is in charge of that particular game. You should get a reminder about the game but it's still good to speak with or Email your game partners making sure you are all aware of the uniform, timing, and transportation. If you get notification from the official in charge, ensure you send a confirmation Email immediately. You don't want to be "that person" whom always needs to be chased after.

Before the game, you'll have a period of time with your crew to prepare. While you're changing into your uniform, the head official will typically talk over things to look for, signals, specific mechanics for specific plays, communication, etc. You'll be able to discuss positioning and crew responsibilities. You'll be able to ask and answer questions about rules or mechanics.

Have a purposeful pregame. When you walk onto the field or court and how you prepare for the game before the kickoff or tipoff will give the coaches and the fans an impression. Don't stand around with your crewmates chatting. Don't warm up in the middle of the field or court. If you have to warm up, be as inconspicuous as possible. Stretch in the end zone or at a corner of the basketball court. (And most definitely, don't bend over to stretch with your backside facing the crowd!) Observe the players and get an idea of what's going on with each of the teams. Some of the things to look for during football warm ups:

- Is the quarterback right handed or left handed?

- How big are the splits on the offensive line?

- What kind of offense and defense do the teams run?

- Who are the dominant physical and athletic players on the field?

- How talented is the kicker and what kind of range does he have?

- Is the kicker right footed or left footed?

- Is the quarterback able to throw down the field effectively?

- Who is wired emotionally and may be a 'hot-head' on the field?

- Are the players legally equipped?

As you observe a basketball pregame, you can look for the following:

- Uniform issues

- Hairpins or earrings that must be removed

- Post play (how adept are the "bigs" as they pivot to the basket?)

- Shooting and dribbling prowess

Your pregame (and paying attention to the small details during the warmup) will help you read your keys better once the game is underway.

HALFTIME

If your sport has a halftime, you'll have the chance to talk about specific plays you saw in the first part of the game. (If an unusual play happens in the first half, write a reminder on your game card or ask your partner to "remember that play" so you can discuss it at half time.) As a new official, you'll want to remain in learning mode. Don't spend the break time attacking or questioning your partners(s). You don't want to walk on the field/court with hard feelings toward each other. Listen and learn and stay away from "yeah but" responses. As we've discussed, no official has worked a perfect game, and there will be plays you'll wish you could "do over." The purpose of the halftime discussion is not to lay blame, but to understand how to better officiate the second half. I've been in locker rooms where two aggressive officials go after each other, and that just serves to bring down the entire crew. If you take a humble approach to the halftime discussions, you'll get more out of them. You may need to discuss how to deal with a coach; sometimes one official had a conversation with a coach that the other officials need to hear. And make sure you hydrate!

POSTGAME

Again, spend this review time to learn! As a new official, your crew partners will most likely have pointed feedback for you. Don't become discouraged if they list multiple mistakes or shortcomings. Remember, you have a steep learning curve and it's inevitable that you'll receive many comments. There may be another crew preparing to work the game after yours, and they may have had the opportunity to watch part of your game. If they have time, ask them for a quick comment. Don't argue or give excuses; just listen. If you don't agree with a comment, just listen and ask clarification questions if you don't understand the feedback. If you work a sub-varsity game outdoors, you probably won't have access to a shower. If you work basketball, you'll probably have an opportunity to shower.

After you get home, jot down some quick notes in a journal. As previously stated, I recommend starting a journal from day one and keeping detailed notes until the day you hang up your whistle. In the journal, write down the following information:

- Date

- Location

- Partners

- Strange plays or notable moments

- What you did well, what you could have done better

- What you learned

The journal is a great way to track your progress as an official.

TRUST YOUR PARTNERS

Depending on the sport and the level, you may be on a crew with one to six additional officials. The number of "eyeballs" available to observe a play will dictate primary coverage areas for each official. When you share a freshman basketball game with one other official or a Junior High football game with two other officials, your primary coverage area will be fairly large (and there will be areas of the field/court that you simply will not be able to view during a play). You'll have to discipline yourself to look "off ball" when appropriate and trust your partners to make the proper calls in their primary coverage areas. Watch a football referee when the quarterback releases the ball on a passing play. He won't turn his head to follow the flight of the ball but will instead keep his eyes trained on the quarterback to look for roughing the passer. Many new officials will watch the ball most of the time, which leaves much of the field/court unattended. As a football wing, when the ball goes away from you, your primary coverage area will be the players behind the play (where "cheap shots" and personal fouls may occur).

I will forever remember a play such as this during my first year. I was officiating an 8-man football game, and the field was more narrow than an 11-man field. A sweep went away from my side of the field, and I kept my eyes directly on the ball carrier who was tackled on the opposite sideline. I observed the defender grasp and pull the runner's facemask, and so I pulled out my flag and attempted to throw it clear across the width of the field. When I reported the foul to the referee, he should have waved off the flag, kicked me in the rear end, and sent me back to my sideline. (When I described the foul to my crew chief, the first question he asked was, "Why were you looking at the ball? Your primary coverage area was behind the ball.") Naturally, the covering official was upset that I was "fishing in his pond," and had to spend some "alone time" cooling off during a subsequent time out.

Everyone on the crew has a specific area to observe as the play unfolds, and it's important to trust your partners to do their jobs. When a football runner breaks away from the pack and races alone into the end zone, only one set of eyes should be on the ball; the rest of the officials should look behind the runner, looking for players hitting defenseless players not involved in the play.

Chapter 10

Game Interactions

INTERACTION AND DEALING WITH CONFLICT

As I mentioned earlier, you are entering a job rife with conflict and disagreement. You can't be offended when conflict surfaces on the field or court, just like an emergency room nurse can't be affronted when he or she is faced with blood and shocking injuries.

When you make a difficult call, it's likely half of the spectators watching the game will be upset because it's against their team. One of the things you should talk to your mentor about is how to deal with conflict. How do you deal with the situation when things don't go right? One of my favorite sayings (an African proverb) is "smooth seas do not make good sailors." Latin writer Publilius Syrus stated, "Anyone can hold the helm when the sea is calm." The implication with these two quotes is that if things always go well, you probably won't learn because of the lack of challenging situations. Frederick Douglass said something very similar, "If there is no struggle, there is no progress." You need to look forward to conflict and difficult plays because they give you an opportunity to get better.

INTERACTING WITH VOLUNTEERS

In some sports, you'll have students or adults assisting with the administration of the event. Some examples include the football chain gang, swimming timers, and volleyball line judges. Some of these assistants may be experienced volunteers that have worked the job for multiple years. Others may be "volun-told" - pulled from the stands under duress - and you'll have to spend a little more time training them and keeping an eye on them during the contest. Don't let the volunteers, especially the teenagers, become distracted with cell phones or by interacting with friends. Also, because these volunteers are part of the officiating crew, they won't be able to cheer or coach. That's especially important with the football chain gang. The home team provides the chain gang, and the chains are set on the visitor's side of the field, resulting in three or four home team fans right in the midst of the visitors' bench area. On multiple occasions I've had to remind the chain crew they are not allowed to create an issue by cheering for the home team, by coaching the players, or by (gasp!) criticizing the football officials. If you feel you need to replace a volunteer, ensure you speak with the official in charge and state your concerns. Sometimes the head official can speak with the offending individuals and improve their behavior.

INTERACTING WITH PLAYERS

You are on the field or court to facilitate and arbitrate a contest organized for student athletes. It's all about them and not you. As stated earlier in the book, if you don't like being around kids, then don't become involved in officiating. One of the least favorite games I officiated was a two-person Middle School intramural football game during my second year. My partner was a veteran official who was visibly agitated with the players the entire game. His tone of voice and body language made it very clear to me - and I'm sure to the players as well - that he didn't want to be on the field. His poor attitude made the game miserable for everyone. I remember thinking, "If you hate doing this, why are you out here?"

Treat the players with respect. I call the players "Sir or Ma'am" and "Gentlemen or Ladies". I try to be as patient as possible within the context of the game. Remember, you're interacting with teenagers who won't have your level of maturity. Parents are advised to not discipline their kids in anger. Similarly, you shouldn't respond in anger to players' actions or words. Give players as much grace as you can while providing appropriate consequences to behavior. Don't instantly respond with a consequence if a player mouths off to you. Obviously, if he or she crosses the line, and especially if the whole gym can hear the comment, you'll probably have to provide the appropriate consequence. But, if you can talk quietly to an agitated player, it will usually de-escalate the situation.

From my experience, Middle and High School athletes will respond positively to a steady influence on the field. Your behavior will help set the tone on the field/court. Use your voice and your physical presence to diffuse potentially volatile situations. Following a held ball on the basketball court or a tackle with a pile of bodies on a football field, use your voice to let the players know you are close. If players "bow up" on each other, voice and proximity will usually help. "You guys are playing a great game - good effort out here - let's just play basketball, all right?" I learned to communicate to football players from Dave "Crusher" Allgood, one of my football mentors. "Use the ground to get up," "Roll off," "Play's over," "Great job gentlemen," were some of the phrases I learned to use. During a preseason scrimmage my first year, I took a turn at the umpire position. Crusher walked over, grabbed my whistle and shoved it in my pocket. "Learn to use your voice," he directed. Obviously, his words were "tongue in cheek," and he really didn't want me to pocket my whistle in a regular season game, but I got his meaning; he wanted me to learn to use my voice to help control the game.

Now for the other side of the coin - you want to convey information to players, but you don't want to be too chatty on the field or court. Use your voice to control and direct the players (create a presence), but don't "coach" the players. Some coaches will be upset if you attempt to give their players advice or instruction. It's not your job to constantly tell players how to perform. Also, be very specific with your words when a player is close to committing a foul. You can warn players, but don't tell the players "That's a hold - if you do that again, I'll flag it." If an opposing coach hears you warn a player with that line, they'll get ticked at you because you didn't throw your flag. A foul is a foul, and if it impacts the play, you need to appropriately enforce the rules. You can communicate with players without implying you turned a blind eye to a foul. "Hey 51, keep your hands inside...if you grab the defender outside his body, that's a hold." On the football field, use the umpire (or the referee if you're using 3-person mechanics) to communicate with linemen. You can tell the umpire to move a lineman back if he's encroaching into the neutral zone.

Players, especially the hot-tempered ones, will complain when they think they are being fouled. When defensive players miss a tackle and the coach yells at them, it's often because "I was held on that play Coach!" In a later section dedicated to interacting with coaches, we'll discuss using questions to control a conversation; the same technique applies to responding to players when they claim they've been fouled. Ask the players for elaborating information and then tell them you'll be on the lookout for that play in the future. As with coaches, you don't have to put up with a constant stream of complaints. I'll never forget a sub-varsity game I Refereed as a newer official. Dennis Wansor, one of my mentors, was the umpire. After a play, it seemed like the entire defensive team clustered around him with an individual complaint about being held, blocked in the back, poked in the eye, etc. With a big grin on his face, Dennis said, "I can only take one complaint at a time. You'll have to take a number." Sometimes humor helps, and in this case, he had all the players laughing with him.

As officials, we often miss the first thing that happens but catch the response from the "offended" player. One player will say something or do something we miss, and then we see the second action from the "offended" player. If I speak to a player about his actions and he complains that he is only reacting to a previous act, I'll candidly say, "I know, you are just reacting to what he/she did. But we (officials) will miss the first thing and will tag you for the second thing we are able to see. I know that's not fair, but that's often what happens." Almost 100% of the time, the player will understand the concept and will calm down. Just like with coaches, the players want to know you are listening to them.

Sometimes you can publicly "call out" a player in an indirect way. Let's say a defensive lineman is angry and won't respond to your private admonishment. You can tell the Umpire (in front of his teammates), "Keep an eye on #56, he's getting agitated out here." Or you can speak to the team captain and request his help to calm the player.

You are not allowed to dictate who gets to play and who has to sit - that's the coach's job. You should never tell a hothead to leave the field or court; you don't have the authority within the rules to do that. As a new official, I observed veteran officials march an agitated player off the field and tell the coach the player "had a brain injury" (implying they were acting like a knucklehead). That's wrong on multiple levels; you don't want to incorrectly imply the player has suffered a physical injury and you don't get to stipulate who gets to play. Unless you've ejected a player, the player has every right to play. If a player is upset and is close to getting out of control, by all means tell the coach. Let the coach know he or she is close to earning a foul for unsportsmanlike conduct. The coach will take care of the player (and will often remove the player from the field or court).

When a player exhibits good sportsmanship, you should make it a point to acknowledge his behavior in front of his teammates. When a player helps an opponent off the ground, I'll thank the player. If the player avoids hitting a defenseless player, or does a good job avoiding hitting the quarterback after he releases a pass, I'll track him down to tell him "great job!" If an opponent pushes him after the play ends and he doesn't retaliate, I'll verbally identify his good behavior in front of his teammates. Also, if a player does something especially noteworthy, make sure you tell the head coach.

Be very careful not to touch players, especially when you are officiating a girl's game. When I work a girl's basketball game and am administering a throw-in, I will hold the ball a foot in front of the player and make her reach out to take the ball from me.

If a player is injured, it is not your job to take care of him or her. Let the medical and coaching staff tend to the player. During an extended injury timeout, allow the players to go to the bench area; you should just move away from the huddle around the injured player and wait. Be careful not to joke around with your fellow officials as others may get the wrong impression (that you are cavalier about the injury). If an ambulance is required, game administration will take care of it.

INTERACTING WITH FANS

Rowdy fans are a part of all high school athletics. "Fan" is short for "Fanatic," and you'll encounter passionate fanatics at most events. You should not address or acknowledge fans before, during, or after a game. There are dozens of incidents around the US where fans confront officials and a verbal or physical altercation takes place. Those situations never end well.

Following a basketball game between two rival schools, my partner and I were confronted by an angry mother who called us names (which happened to be somewhat amusing). We just kept walking. I had a fan confront us as we exited the field after a high school football game to complain about the personal fouls we had called against his team. Never mind his team had won the game 42-12 and we had been in a running clock for most of the second half. He wanted to remind us "this isn't ballet, it's football!" I can't think of a single comment to provide to satisfy a fan like that. (Although when he said "I want your names!", I was sorely tempted to respond, "Why, you don't like the name your mother gave you?")

If a fan approaches you, be polite and professional. If a fan asks you a question, you can answer it, but if you sense the fan is going to start an argument, you can politely say "our association's policy is not to interact with fans." Most schools will provide security to walk you to/from the court/field to the locker room. If you have an unruly fan that is disruptive during the game, you should find the game administrator and let him or her deal with the fan.

You'll be able to hear people yelling from the stands criticizing your calls; just ignore them and give no indication that you can hear them or are affected by their words. You're not there to please everyone. You're there to officiate the best game you can and by the nature of your job, your calls will be unpopular with a large portion of the fans. Many fans don't understand the rule differences between what they see on TV at the college and NFL level and what they see on Friday night at a high school football game and there is nothing you can do to fix that.

INTERACTING WITH YOUR PARTNERS

In the majority of sports, you will not be the sole individual officiating the game. Learn how to say 'we' and 'us' instead of 'I' and 'me.' Remember, you are a team. Talk to your mentor about interacting with other members of your crew. You'll have partners that are strong and partners that are weak. Your weak partners may lack rules knowledge or be out of shape and and maybe can't get in position to make the best call. They might even treat the players poorly or insert themselves into a game where they shouldn't. Some officials will brag about "whacking" a coach. They don't have the patience or the maturity to work through a problem with a coach without throwing a flag or giving a technical foul. You're still a team, so you need to remain neutral and support your partners. Never talk poorly about a fellow official to a coach or player, even if you vehemently disagree with his or her behavior. Never tell a coach, "That's not my call," because you're implying your partner missed something you and the coach observed. If you experience a problem with a fellow official, you can discuss the issue with your mentor or crew chief when you get home.

It is imperative you are consistent as an official and as a crew. Consistency begins at the state association level with association guidelines and policies. Ensure you read all correspondence from the state association; visit their website and look for bulletins and directives. Your state and local football officials associations will then publish guidelines and policies that will obviously be in line with the state principles. Then you'll have policies from your crew chief (if you have one) and specific game referee or lead official. All of the direction and guidelines you get from your "leadership" will help you be consistent with the other officials in your state, association, and crew. Coaches love it when they get consistent officiating, when they know where their boundaries lay. It's not fair to a basketball coach if during one game, they can wander far from the coach's box without warning or penalty and during another game, they get a quick technical foul for the same behavior. It's obvious we're not exactly the same as officials, and that the coaches will have to adjust from game to game, but the more consistency we can provide to the coaches, the better. This applies to similar plays in a single game. A block/charge decision in a basketball game must be the same on both ends of the floor if the plays are similar. If one wing passes on a potential defensive pass interference call, the other wing can't throw a flag on a similar play. One wing can't let his sideline's coach come out to the numbers to talk to the quarterback while the other wing makes his coach stay on the sideline. Pregame discussion and discussion during the game (during timeouts) and at halftime are essential to ensure you are consistent as a crew.

Be prepared to take criticism from your partners during and after the game. You'll work with hundreds of officials over the course of your career so be prepared to work with all sorts of people with all types of personalities. You'll quickly be able to find officials with whom you work well (and may be willing to become your mentor). Learn as much as you can from the veterans but don't follow the advice of all officials blindly. It is very possible (depending on your effort and ability) that you'll have better rules knowledge than an official that has been working games for decades. Listen to everyone respectfully and then ask someone that you trust and esteem what they think. Ultimately, don't allow personality conflicts to get in the way of learning. If you hear something that doesn't seem quite right, write it down in your journal and ask your mentor about it. If you don't have a mentor yet, look the up the rule interpretation when you get home or post a question on an officiating forum to seek other opinions.

UNDER CONSTANT OBSERVATION

Everyone owns a smartphone and you'll see many video cameras in the stands during games. You'll be recorded from every angle during the game, and you'll sometimes hear from coaches or parents following the game about a call you missed that was verified by their "instant replay." In fact, you might even get that feedback during the game.

During a semi-pro football game, one of the coaches said his quarterback had been facemasked during a tackle. I hadn't observed the facemask and the coach wasn't angry, so we moved on to the next play. A few minutes later, the coach approached me with a camera and a huge grin on his face. He showed me a picture of his quarterback with a defender's hand clearly grasping and twisting the facemask - completely obvious in freeze frame.

In this information age, you may find yourself on the 5 O'Clock News or on a Youtube clip. Be cognizant that every move you make will be recorded; conduct yourself with this reality in mind. Also, do not use social media (i.e., Facebook or Twitter) to comment on games you worked. In the information age, assume anything you post will be viewed by everyone.

INTERACTING WITH COACHES

At the beginning of this chapter, there is a paragraph about interacting and dealing with conflict. While there is a modicum of conflict between the fans and officials or the players and officials, the majority of the conflict an official faces is directly with a coach. You may have noticed that we didn't discuss coach interaction in this chapter. That's because there's so much to explore on the topic that an entire chapter is dedicated to the issue. You'll find in-depth coverage of coach interaction in the next chapter.

Chapter 11
Interacting with Coaches

INTERACTING WITH COACHES

In my third year of football officiating, my new crew chief called me on the phone to tell me I would be his top varsity linesman. He gave me two specific directives: 1) Take care of your sideline, and 2) Don't throw BS flags. I will always remember his phone call as it summarized much of a wing's responsibilities on the football field. Obviously, we have other duties and functions, but it was clear to me one of my primary responsibilities was sideline management.

Coaches have invested hundreds of hours in the game you are officiating. They spend hours on the practice field, game planning, watching film, and accomplishing many other tasks. Like it or not, wins and losses do matter, even at the high school level. Ray Lutz gave me a perspective I'll never forget: The junior and high school athletic coach is in a unique position because his or her "performance" is available for everyone to observe and assess. The drama or forensics coach or band teacher may also put his or her "product" on display, but in the vast majority of cases, his or her job is not on the line if results do not meet expectations. The athletic coach's "product" is visible, and the stakes are often very high and a coach's job is often on the line. Emotions will often run high due to the investment of time and effort and the consequences of poor performance.

CONTROL

As Randy Campbell observes, most head coaches are accustomed to being in control of pretty much everything all of the time. In 2014, college coaches were the highest-paid state employees in 40 states and the level of control and authority they exercised matched their income. That's not true of high school coaches, but many head coaches from successful programs are familiar with having unquestioned authority and control in their athletic environment. So what drives coaches crazy? In practice, coaches have control. However, when you shake a coach's hand during the pregame conversation, control and authority is shifted to the official. In a way, coaches may feel they've surrendered control of game. The key is how you as an official handle the control.

EMOTION

As such, give the coaches some grace when interacting with them on the sidelines during a game. Do not allow your emotion or ego to create a problem. Keep a level head and your emotions on an even keel. A soft answer does turn away wrath. Don't match volume with volume, and don't draw attention to yourself with your voice or actions. It's hard for a coach to maintain a high level of anger when you respond in a calm voice.

INFLUENCE

Some coaches will get on you from the beginning just to see how you will respond. If a coach can intimidate you, he or she may be able to get a favorable call from you later in the game. Don't become angry at the coaches for trying to influence how you call the game. That's just the nature of the environment in which you operate. (We've all watched games on TV where the announcer mentions the coaches are "working" the officials.) Let the coaches know with your calm and confident demeanor you will work hard for them and will call the game fairly and consistently. Don't let a coach's anger influence your next call. Don't make a call against a coach because you're angry and don't make a call for a coach because you're intimidated.

NEUTRALITY

When you interact with coaches, don't give the impression of favoritism. If you appear "chummy" with coaches, players, or fans, the opposing team may believe you will favor them during the game. Avoid spending too much time with coaches in the pregame introductions. You want to have a thorough pregame with the coaches, but you don't want to loiter. This also applies when interacting with the table at a basketball or lacrosse game. If you act too familiar with the table personnel, the visiting coach may think he or she will be the victim of "home cooking" during the game. Also, avoid using too much levity when interacting with coaches. Sometimes humor can diffuse a tense situation, but be wary of giving coaches the impression you are goofing off or are not taking the game seriously. You can definitely add fuel to a fire by joking around at the wrong time.

INVOKE THE RULE BOOK

When you speak with an agitated coach, try to explain your decisions by invoking the rule book. It's easy for a coach to argue with you; it's much harder for the coach to argue with the rule book. Coaches may not understand the rules, and they may be agitated when you properly follow the rules. When you speak to a coach, say "By rule," and then state exactly what the rule book says. Words matter, so try to memorize the specific words for important rules. For example, many coaches don't understand the football horse-collar rule. They'll see a runner grabbed by the collar and dragged forward or they'll see a runner jerked back by the back of the pads but not taken to the ground and they'll demand a flag for a horse collar foul. You can say, "Coach, by rule, it is a horse collar if the defender pulls the runner backward or sideward to the ground. The defender pulled the runner forward so, by rule, it is not a horse collar." Or, "the runner was not pulled to the ground, so, by rule, it is not a horse collar."

BACK TO THE BENCH

If a coach comes onto the court or field to dispute a call, calmly escort the coach back to the sideline. Have the conversation in front of the bench, and not out in the middle of an open area. Be aware of the times you need to communicate with both coaches (in girl's lacrosse, any "formal" conversation must be in the presence of both coaches). You don't always have to include both coaches, and it's okay to speak with each coach individually, but you don't want to leave one coach "hanging" if he or she is unsure of what is going on.

LET THE COACH COME TO YOU

Very rarely do you want to initiate a conversation with a coach. Don't invite trouble. If the coach is just making comments, and he's not showing you up or being overly demonstrative, just let him be. If you are the kind of person who always has to have the last word, or if you are the kind of person who always has to explain him/herself, you'll have a hard time on the sideline. Let a coach vent and then give him or her the opportunity to disengage. Don't chase a coach to explain yourself.

A few years ago, I worked a football game where the coach approached our crew at halftime to vent his frustration with a few calls we had made. He was very angry and complained about the comportment of one of the wing officials. He threatened to contact the state association. He then started walking away. The official that worked his sideline called after him and said, "You can't just yell at us and then walk away. You need to give us an opportunity to respond." I stopped the official and said, "yes Joe (not his real name), we do want him to walk away. We don't need to respond. Let him go."

Very rarely do I leave a contest where both coaches are pleased with the crew. That's just the nature of the profession you've chosen. If you insist on making sure the coach completely understands why you made a specific decision, you're inviting trouble. Understand you will often depart a contest without closure on every conflict; if you are the type of person who needs everyone to get along, prepare to be disappointed. If you approach a coach simply to explain yourself, you're asking for a confrontation and you'll be the one at fault for re-igniting a fire that was starting to go out.

ASKING 'THE QUESTION'

If you see a coach is agitated, and you feel you need to speak to him, start the conversation with "Coach, what's your concern?" That's a great way to start the conversation. Don't assume you understand the reason he's upset. Steven Covey authored a book titled The Seven Habits of Highly Effective People. One of the habits is "Seek first to understand, then to be understood." Most of the time you speak to a coach, it is to understand his concern and to let him know you are listening and attentive. So you'll want to ask questions. Randy Campbell has taught me a lot about interacting with coaches. One of the things he says is "the person who asks the questions controls the conversation." For example, if a football coach is yelling "he's holding!" you can ask the following questions:

- "Coach what did you see"? (He's holding my guy!)

- "Can you describe the action"? (He grabbed my guy's jersey!)

- "What number"? (Number 12)

- "I got it coach" (Well, aren't you going to call it?)

- "Coach, let me share with you what I observed"

If a coach is making a statement, determine whether or not that statement needs a response. Statements or questions like the following do not require a response:

- How could you miss that call?

- What were you looking at?

- That's the worst call I've ever seen.

- That's a hold!

Some coaches will keep up a running commentary about your crew's performance for the entire game. Candidly, with the "always agitated" coach, it's difficult to separate the "wheat from the chaff" and pick out the legitimate concerns. Other coaches will barely speak to you over the course of the game. If one of the "quiet most of the time" coaches has a comment or becomes agitated, make it a point to get to him or her as quickly as possible to hear the concern.

In soccer, the referees don't have time to start (and sustain) a conversation. There are not a lot of breaks in the action where officials can have a lengthy conversation with coaches and the fluid nature of the game demandes minimal interference from coaches. Soccer coaches have obligations; one is to allow for the flow of the game (the clock only stops in high school soccer for injury, penalty kick, after a goal is scored, and at the end of periods). So soccer officials are instructed to follow the "ask, tell, dismiss" approach when dealing with unacceptable behavior:

- Ask the person to modify his or her behavior - if the behavior doesn't stop, then...

- Tell the person his or her actions will not be tolerated and tell him or her to stop - if the inappropriate behavior doesn't stop, then...

- Take the final step in the process and dismiss the person from the field of play

PAY ATTENTION

If the coach wants information about why you made a call, you should address that question. Coaches want to know that you're paying attention to them. You can achieve this through good eye contact, verbal confirmations like "I hear you coach" or "I understand," and honesty. There are some plays where my eyes see a foul, but my mouth doesn't get the signal from my brain to exhale. There are plays where it's obvious to everyone in the gym but me that a foul or violation has occurred.

Just last year I was working a girl's basketball playoff game. As trail official, I was "on ball" and was conducting a 10 second count as the point guard dribbled the ball upcourt. She was close to her opponent's bench and was not being guarded, so I stole a quick glance at the clock and at the girls who were preparing to trap the dribbler at the division line. At that very moment, for some inexplicable reason, the girl picked up her dribble and took two halting steps right in front of the opposing coach. And I wasn't watching! The coach lept off the bench like he had been stung, and the visiting crowd hooted and howled. The worse thing was, the girl "gave herself up" by hanging her head in disgust...everyone in the gym but me knew she had committed a violation. I should have blown the whistle based on the girl's reaction, but I didn't.

You'll experience plays like that, especially in your first few years when you are getting used to the pace of the game. Be willing to admit it if you blew a call. If you didn't see a play but you're pretty sure you missed it, you can say, "Coach, if what you described happened, I missed it." Coaches don't want to hear you constantly apologizing for missing calls, but they appreciate your willingness to be honest when you boot something. You really have to develop a short memory after missing a call. Don't agonize or grieve over your mistakes. You must put that mistake in the rear-view mirror and move on. If you spend any brain-bytes thinking about the call you just missed, you might not clearly see the play happening real-time right in front of you. You'll hear veteran officials say, "The day I work a perfect game, I'm going to retire!" Those officials know they will make mistakes, and they are able to move on to the next play.

Don't Pass the Buck

Often, a coach will yell at you because he or she is agitated about a play that was in front of one of your partners. Don't let it rattle you when you are yelled at for something that is completely out of your control. That's the nature of the job. Remember, you are not individuals on the field or court, you are a team. Use "we" as much as possible in your responses. Never throw your partner under the bus by saying "That's not my call." That implies your partner was wrong and you would have made the call if the play was in your primary coverage area. It's okay to tell a coach you weren't looking at the area where the perceived foul occurred, but don't say it in a way that implies your partner missed a call. It's okay to go through your series of questions to understand the coach's concern. If the coach wants defensive pass interference on the other side of the field, I might say to a coach, "What did you see from way over here? My partner had a really good look at that play." If the coach still needs an explanation, tell the coach, "I'll find out for you," and then get an answer for the coach as soon as practical (don't stop or slow down the game to get an explanation). Don't allow a coach to yell across the field/court at one of your partners. Tell the coach you'll get an answer for him/her; it's okay to say "Coach, you can't yell across the field/court. I'll get you an answer." In football, you can wait for a timeout, for a quarter or halftime break, or you can relay the question through the referee or umpire. The coaches want to know you are listening to them, so they will appreciate when you get an answer quickly. In basketball, the officials rotate to different positions on the court, so you can tell the coach, "I don't know the answer to that question, but my partner will rotate in front of you and you'll be able to ask him/her."

ASSISTANT COACHES

You don't have to take grief from assistant coaches. If an assistant coach is upset and is yelling at you, you can calmly address the coach and ask for help with the assistant. You can say, "Coach, I'm happy to talk with you, but I need your help with your assistant." The same applies to unruly players. Instead of confronting the player, let the head coach or an assistant coach deal with him or her. "Coach, I need your help with #23." As Randy Campbell notes, head coaches were formerly assistant coaches, so you don't want to disregard assistants; they may one day become head coaches. You want to respect assistant coaches just as you respect head coaches. If you burn a bridge with an assistant coach, you may have to one day work with him or her as a head coach.

GRACE UNDER PRESSURE

As alluded to earlier, if you know you missed a call, allow the coach to vent (as long as he or she is not profane or overly demonstrative). Don't let the coach show you up, but give the coach room to voice his or her displeasure. You just missed a call, and you really can't expect a coach to always react calmly. The more veteran coaches understand officials are fallible, and they'll give you grace, but you may work for a coach that won't give you that grace. Don't add fuel to the fire by penalizing a coach for responding to your mistake with a little emotion. There is no "one size fits all" rule to follow, every official will have a different "tolerance level," and every situation will be different. If the coach is overly demonstrative to the point where everyone in the stands can see that he or she has crossed the line, then a penalty is absolutely warranted. I've heard some officials talk about a "compilation rule" where one single comment doesn't warrant a penalty, but a compilation of minor complaints will eventually push the coach over the line to receive a technical foul or unsportsmanlike conduct foul. I'm not a big fan of that philosophy; you need to develop the ability to work with a coach throughout the entire game without reaching a breaking point. If you can take a single comment, you should be able to put up with a series of comments. I'm not saying you should allow coaches to walk all over you and harass you the entire game. In my opinion, it takes more skill and courage to work with a coach to get through a rough stretch than to just "whack" a coach because you've had enough. If you've reached your limit, let the coach know (we call that giving the coach the "stop sign"). You can say, "Coach, I've heard your concern and I understand what you're saying. It's time to move on. We're done discussing that issue." It's okay to tell a coach "that's enough." You just don't have to do it with a consequence.

Also, if it's just you and the coach having a "personal" conversation, then you'll have to decide what is too much. In my opinion, a coach can pretty much say anything if it's just between us. The fans, players, and assistant coaches have no idea if he's questioning my parentage or if we're exchanging dessert recipes. If a coach says something that is inappropriate, simply say, "Coach, do you mind repeating what you just said, because I'm not sure I heard you right." That gives him or her a chance to back-peddle and take a different tact. Everyone will have a breaking point where they finally award a penalty to the coach for inappropriate behavior. I've seen officials "whack" a coach for saying "C'mon, how can you miss that?" or "You need to call it both ways!" or for jumping in the air when a foul wasn't called. In my opinion, that official's fuse was a little too short.

You'll also have to make a decision if the coach exhibits unsportsmanlike behavior that is not directed toward you. In my second year of football officiating, I overheard a coach encourage his players to hurt an opposing player. I've also had coaches yell across the field to the opposing coach at the end of a blowout game because they were upset about the opposing coach running up the score. In both of those examples, it's appropriate for the official to step in to correct the behavior. If you overhear the coach encouraging unsportsmanlike behavior, a simple way to nip it in the bud is to step into the huddle and say (in the presence of his players), "Coach, I thought I might have heard you encourage your players to purposefully hurt the opponent. I'm sure I didn't hear that right because that would be inappropriate."

You'll run into coaches at the lower levels that must believe the NFL or NBA will call them tomorrow to offer them a job. They yell at the officials because they see coaches on television (college or professional level) yell at officials and get away with it. The college and professional "culture" is much different than the junior high and high school culture and much of the behavior you witness on TV is simply not tolerated at the lower levels. If you encounter an immature coach who simply doesn't "get it," you can say, "Coach, we're not doing this today. If you have an issue, we can chat quietly, but I'm not going to allow you to act like this. We can have a conversation and I'll be happy to listen to your concerns."

Sometimes a coach will be upset with you because you ruled on a play correctly and he or she had an officiating crew rule on the play differently in a previous game. This is where perfect rules knowledge will come in handy.

A few years ago I worked a football playoff game that quickly turned into a rout. In the fourth quarter, the visiting team was behind by six touchdowns with only a few seconds remaining in the game. Predictably, they chose not to punt on fourth down and 10 yards to go. The quarterback scrambled to the right and ran directly out of bounds well short of the line-to-gain. After stepping out of bounds, one of the defensive backs cut him down below the knees. Both I (as the referee) and the linesman threw flags for a personal foul. I reported on the microphone that the runner had not reached the line-to-gain, the personal foul was a dead-ball foul, so it was the home team's football. We would mark off 15 yards from the dead ball spot and it would be first and 10 for the home team. The visiting team's head coach was very upset and wanted us to award him 15 yards and a first down. He claimed "that same play" had happened twice in the regular season and the officiating crew had awarded them a first down. I responded, "Coach, I'm not familiar with the previous plays, but by rule, your quarterback did not reach the line-to-gain and so the ball is turned over on downs. The 15 yard penalty is marked off from the succeeding spot and the other team gets the ball." The head coach was still not happy after my explanation. Of course, the visiting team's fans booed us as well.

If a coach ever mentions a call by another crew, don't throw those officials "under the bus." Simply state, "I'm not familiar with the play you described, but by rule…"

Coaches may complain that you missed a call based on information the coach received from an assistant coach in the press box. Or in a game later in the season, a coach may comment that he watched game film and saw a play you missed. Randy Campbell gives great advice on how to respond to those complaints. Typically, video equipment and assistant coaches in the press box are located 20-50 feet above field or court level. Remind the coach most officials are between 5'5" and 6'5" in height and don't have that great angle from 20-50 feet above the play. It would be nice to have an official in the press box with a microphone who could call down to the field and say "throw your flag, I see a hold," but obviously that isn't part of the game. You have a court/field level view, and if you move to improve your look between players, that's the best view you'll get.

RULE IGNORANCE

You'll get much of your grief from coaches and especially fans because they just don't understand the rules. As you dig through the rule book, you'll understand why that is often true. (Try to explain Post Scrimmage Kick enforcement or the Momentum Exception to Force to a parent and then decide if I'm speaking the truth.) Also, fans and coaches will watch an NFL or college game on television, then yell because we throw a flag or don't throw a flag on a particular play. A few of my "favorite" misunderstandings: A high school quarterback cannot intentionally throw the ball away, even if he's outside the tackle box. Encroaching defensive linemen cannot jump back to avoid a foul. 12 men in the huddle is not a foul. You can still have defensive pass interference, even if the pass is uncatchable. There is no "halo" rule during scrimmage kicks. Those are only a few of the rule misunderstandings you'll encounter during a high school football game. When the parents yell, there's really not much you can do. But when a coach doesn't understand a rule, you can politely inform him of what the rule book says about the play. "Coach, that's not a high school rule," is a statement I'll make at many of the football games I work, especially at the sub-varsity level. Remember the "by rule" statement.

Many states and associations have conduct guidelines for coaches and players. The Colorado High School Activities Association publishes very specific guidelines regarding conduct of players, coaches, and fans. If you have any questions, you should contact your crew chief or your association leadership. Know what you need to report if any problems happen during a game like a personal foul or ejection. If you have issues during a game, your state or local association may require a special game report describing the incidents. You'll probably need to provide names in your report, so ensure you get that information from the coach or from the scorer's table before the game ends and you exit the field or court.

Especially at the beginning of a game, there may be opportunities to "put money in the bank" with a head coach. In football, counting players and letting a coach know he has too many or too few players on the field is an example. Letting a defensive coach know one of his lineman needs to move back a smidge on the line is another example. At the junior high level, you'll have plenty of opportunities to "make deposits," especially at the beginning of the season. This doesn't mean you should ignore blatant fouls, and as we discussed earlier, your job is not to coach the players. "Putting money in the bank" simply means there may be opportunities during the game to inform the coach of minor issues that didn't impact the outcome of the play. When you put money in the bank with a coach, you can then make a withdrawal (a call "against" the coach) without the coach thinking you are out to get him or her.

Chapter 12
Development and Progression as an Official

ADVANCING IN YOUR ASSOCIATION

Your personality, perseverance, determination, and passion will be noticed by veteran officials in your association. Always be respectful of others' opinions and be teachable and coachable. Try to build meaningful relationships with veterans. Always be on time. You'll quickly get a reputation if you are consistently late. If you're going to be even 5 minutes late, pick up the phone and call. It will be appreciated. Communication is key. If you get an Email requesting information or requiring a response, send a response back right away. Don't be the person that needs to be nagged or checked on. Take initiative. Even new officials can be part of the process of making other officials better. You might be able to teach a new officials class during your second or third season. Volunteer to provide a rules quiz during your association's meetings. Teaching others is a great way to learn yourself. Be vocal but don't be annoying. Watch as many varsity games (including sitting in on pregames) as your schedule allows. Work as many games as you can to gain on field experience. The number of games you work is directly related to your development as an official. If someone is able to work more games or is able to work a varsity game before you, don't think poorly of them. Don't use your fellow officials as traction on your way to the top. They may have had opportunities you didn't or may have worked harder to get to their position in the association. Don't be "that guy" who believes he's destined to work in the NFL or NBA in the near future. Availability is often a contributing factor with regard to official development. The more available you are, the more games you can work. The more games you work, the more experience you'll gain and the better your chances will be to work higher level games in the future.

CAMPS

Try to attend camps in the off-season. Camps will help you stay focused on your development; you'll also receive valuable feedback from veteran or college-level officials. Ask your mentor or a respected member in your association about prospective camps. Ask younger officials about their recent camp experiences. A new basketball official will surely benefit from attending the IAABO camp which is offered across the country. When you attend a camp or clinic, you'll hear a plethora of information and some advice may seem to conflict. The clinicians will most likely acknowledge this and will tell you to focus on a little at a time and not to try to incorporate everything at once.

ART AND SCIENCE OF OFFICIATING

Officiating is both an "art" and a "science." The "science" is the rules part of officiating and is written in black and white. However, some rules are open to interpretation, and that's where the "art" comes into play. For example, what constitutes "holding" in football? You've probably heard there is holding on every play; although you won't see holding on every play, you'll see action that meets the technical definition of holding on many plays that is (correctly) not flagged. The rule book is very specific about the definition of holding and you'll hear "That's holding!" from the sideline and stands on multiple plays during a game. It will take practice, lots of reps on the field, hours of conversations with respected officials, and many hours of film study to become adept at discerning action that deserves a flag and action that will not be penalized.

IT'S ON YOU

Your individual effort and development is ultimately your responsibility. You may be one member of a crew or larger organization but it's not the organization's job to develop you into a quality veteran official. The organization's job is to get you started and provide resources to help you succeed. It's your hard work, drive, initiative, and determination that will help you grow into a good official.

IT TAKES TIME

Ronald E. Osborn said, "Unless you try to do something beyond what you have already mastered, you will never grow." It takes only a few days or weeks to for a weed to grow. It takes years for a tree to grow. Which one do you want to be, the weed or the sturdy tree? As time passes, it's essential to balance the confidence you'll need to constantly progress in the association with the humbleness required to fully develop at each level.

I remember in my first year of football officiating desperately wanting to work a varsity game. The association sent out an Email looking for officials to travel to a distant location to work a lower-level varsity game. I sent a message to my crew chief asking to be scheduled for the game. His response was disappointing, but was 100% correct. He affirmed my development and stated I was progressing very well as a first year official. However, he stated I needed to see a lot more snaps at the sub-varsity level before I would be ready to be an efficient varsity official. He wasn't questioning my desire or commitment; I just needed to see more plays. I continued to work hard and was able to referee the final sub-varsity game of the year.

It's important to realize success is not necessarily the number or level of games you work. Depending on where you officiate, you may not work a varsity game for many years. Some associations have fixed crews, and you will just have to wait your turn to be "assimilated" into the veteran pool. Other associations are desperate for officials and you may find yourself working a varsity game your first season. So, just focus on what you can control. You can strive to be the best rules person in your association. You can work on your physical fitness. And you can spend as many nights as your family will allow attending games and watching other officials. Contribute and participate in online forums. Read articles, magazines, and blogs related to officiating. Trust me, the veteran officials will notice and will appreciate your enthusiasm and hard work.

VIDEO REVIEW

Watching film can accelerate your development as an official. In your first few years, you may not get the opportunity to see yourself on video as you will most likely be working sub-varsity games that may not be filmed. Of course, this depends on the state in which you officiate. Try to figure out a way to get some of your officiating time on tape; there is no better tool than to watch yourself on tape (and to have someone else watch the tape with you and critique your performance). With today's video technology, it's not that hard to find someone to tape you for at least a quarter or two. Ask a family member or a friend to record your game. If you can't have someone tape your games, view games worked by other officials.

There are two basic types of Video Review:

1. Video of you

2. Video of other officials

There are benefits for each type. When you watch yourself on film, you are able to see the game from a new perspective (and typically from a slightly higher angle). You are able to determine if you made the right call on a bang-bang play. "Hindsight is 20/20" so video review can ease any doubts you may have had about a particular call. It also allows you to answer question like:

- Am I looking in the right areas and reading the right keys?

- Are my mechanics correct and is my positioning appropriate?

- Did I miss any calls I should have made? If so, why didn't I get them?

- What do I need to work on?

When you watch games other officials worked, you are able to observe behavior that should be emulated or avoided. It isn't a contest between you and the official on the tape. Your attitude should never be "I'm a better official than _____." Analyze their mechanics and calls. Are they in the right position? Do they do things you should be doing? Use your critical thinking skills and extract what's both good and bad from their performance. Film study is beneficial, because it's not live action. You can rewind a play, study it in slow motion, and even watch a game at 1.5 or 2X speed. The more action you see, the better prepared you will be when the same situation happens to you. Watch film of veteran officiating crews or of a level you aspire to reach. Watch high-level high school officials, college-level officials, and professional-level officials (understand the mechanics at each level might be slightly different). There's a reason they're officiating at that high level. Strive to emulate their good habits.

Again, ask a veteran official to watch the games with you and point out proper and improper positioning and mechanics. Tell the veteran official to be very specific (nit-pick) with his or her comments. You want to know what right looks like so you can emulate proper behavior and avoid improper behavior.

Goals

It is always a good idea to set goals and track them. Set short-, mid-, and long-term goals. Ensure they are measurable and realistic. "Be a better official" is not measurable; "Score 95% or better on my rules test" is measurable. "Work a state championship by my fifth year" is not realistic. "White-hat a sub-varsity game during my third year" is realistic. If you need help setting your goals, ask your mentor or a veteran you trust and respect. They will have a good idea of what your realistic expectations should be. Write the goals down and review them periodically. Then figure out actions you'll need to take to reach those goals.

Officiating at the College Level

If one of your goals is to become a college official, I would highly recommend Todd Skaggs' book Forward Progress. He discusses what it takes to get to the next level of officiating. You can read more about his book at www.artofofficiating.com/Forward-Progress-Book

Chapter 13
Parting Words

I sincerely hope this book has provided tangible information that will assist you in your officiating development. I encourage you to treat officiating as a true profession and not just a part-time hobby. A serious high school athlete will not wait until the day before the first game of the season to dust off his/her equipment and finally pay attention to preparing for the season. Dedicated athletes will lift weights in the off-season, attend camps, attend multiple practices and study the playbook. Unfortunately, I've observed some officials who are satisfied to attend one state clinic, maybe attend a preseason scrimmage, and then step on the field or court to officiate a high school varsity game. Those officials are in the minority, but they're out there. Don't be that official...take the time to attend a camp or clinic in the off-season. Keep your nose in the rule book (commit yourself to be your association's top "rules guy"). Remain physically fit. Visit officiating web sites and read other officials' stories and game accounts. Watch video and observe how officials conduct themselves. Look at their positioning and how they react to specific plays. Don't be satisfied to stay at the same level; always strive to improve.

Chapter 14
My History with Sports

I've always loved sports and competition is a large part of my identity. My earliest memories are of playing baseball, kickball, and touch-football in the backyard in Massachusetts. As a pre-teen, my parents let me watch one hour of television each day, and I would save up my hours to watch a baseball game on the weekend. I grew up on the island of Guam in the South Pacific, and when I was 12 years old, I traveled to Taiwan to play in the Far East Little League baseball tournament. Each year, the tournament winner would send a team to Williamsport, Pennsylvania to represent the Far East in the Little League World Series. I pitched against Korea and got hammered...as I recall, the final score was 19-2. I played basketball and baseball in junior high school and football, basketball, and baseball in high school.

I attended Whitworth College, a small liberal arts school in Spokane, Washington, and chose to major in Physical Education so I could be involved in coaching, athletics, and teaching at the junior high or high school level. My sophomore year in college, a friend and I decided to try officiating basketball. That first year, I officiated mostly at the junior high school level as an apprentice. There wasn't much formal training for the rookies; we met in one room as a large association and the veteran officials talked about rules and plays with each other. The rookies just sat around wondering what was going on. We had very little mechanics training; I now wonder how in the world I knew what to do on the court. I worked one junior varsity high school game that season and remember the thrill I felt as the fans started to arrive prior to the varsity game, providing a little more emotion and noise to the normally quiet sub-varsity game. The band also arrived and played a few fight songs to add even more excitement. While a student in college, I directed the college intramural programs and officiated a few of the intramural sports. I also did radio play-by-play for basketball and worked a few football games as the radio color guy. During my senior year in college, I completed my student teaching at Mead High School near Spokane, Washington. One of my tenth grade physical education students was Jason Hanson, who was the Detroit Lions' place kicker for 21 years.

After graduation, the men's Varsity basketball coach at Whitworth College asked me to resurrect the junior varsity program, so I became the head coach, scheduler, launderer, bus driver, and video guy for the JV college basketball team. We didn't have any other small college JV teams in the area, so I filled the schedule with adult men's rec league teams. The next summer, I went to Air Force Officer Training School and began my career as a Missile Launch Officer at Minot Air Force Base, North Dakota. I played every intramural sport possible: football, basketball, softball, racquetball, volleyball, and even bowling. I was the head coach of Minot Air Force Base's softball team and continued to participate in athletics throughout the year. I also enjoyed coaching my son's and daughter's youth sports teams.

MY LOVE OF COMPETITION

I love to compete. I'll compete in anything...who can hold their breath the longest underwater, who can hit the most free throws, who can win the most games of pool...I like seeing who the best person is at a particular game. Just playing "for fun" isn't as enjoyable because I have to have a winner and a loser. Playing a video game against the computer Artificial

Intelligence isn't as fun as playing against another human because I want to compete against a real person. "I'll bet you a soda" was, and still is, a common phrase I use when I want to initiate a competition or challenge.

I have to confess, I lived vicariously through my son James as he played sports as a teenager. I enjoyed participating as a spectator. James was a successful football player, and during the workweek I always looked forward to his Friday night game. We moved quite a bit in the Air Force and for my son's eighth grade through tenth grade years, we lived in Niceville, Florida. Before we moved to the new town, I called the Junior High school secretary to glean some information about the school my kids would attend. I asked the school secretary if they had a football team. I'll never forget her reply; in a southern drawl she answered, "Son, this is the South!" James was all-conference in eighth grade and started his high school Freshman season on the junior varsity squad. Because of injuries, James was promoted as a Freshman to varsity long-snapper the week of Homecoming. Niceville has a rich football tradition, and it was common for thousands of fans to attend the varsity games. James' first varsity snap came on fourth down with the ball at midfield. I remember the butterflies I felt as he ran onto the field. He lined up and fired a bullet, but over the punter's head! A few series later, Niceville faced fourth down from their own 1 yard line. The punter stood with his heels right in front of the back line of the end zone. I felt like I was going to throw up. I turned to my wife and croaked, "If James snaps it over the punter's head, we are going to have to move." This time, James drilled the snap to the punter's chest. Throughout his high school "career," James developed his snapping skill so that I no longer feared fourth down. His senior year in Colorado Springs, James earned All-Conference honors as an offensive lineman. As you can probably tell, each game was an exciting event for me as James found success on the gridiron.

It wasn't just the football game that thrilled me. I enjoyed the bands playing and the large cheering crowds. I enjoyed the National Anthem and the pomp and circumstance of high school football, especially during the homecoming game. After my son graduated from high school, it seemed like there was something missing. I still played softball on a local church team, but I yearned to be part of a sporting event on a bigger stage. We were stationed in Korea for two years, and when I returned in 2006, I decided to become involved with athletics as an official. I was becoming too old to keep up with the younger athletes on the softball field and the basketball court, so I thought officiating would be a great way to continue to stay connected to sports and "compete" in a new way.

Appendix A
Tips for New Football Officials

The following is a document I put together for our new football officials. I might be useful for you.

Note: Officiating is both an "art" and a "science." The "science" is rule and mechanics knowledge; you must know the rule book "cold." When you step onto the field, coaches, players, admin and spectators trust that you have prepared yourself properly to officiate the game. They don't know if this is your very first game or your 300th game – they put time and effort to prepare for the game and so should you. As a wing, you are standing on the sideline and will need to communicate properly with coaches, players and chain crew. Do not rely on your crew partners to be your "safety net" for rule knowledge. The "art" of officiating is being able to administer the game properly within the context of the rule book. Your crew chief (in general) and your white hat (Referee or R) for each game will be the final arbiter on your role as a wing and on how the crew will function.

OVERALL

- Be "teachable!" You're a new official and will learn a lot of new information each time you officiate. Don't be offended when you're corrected before/during/after a game.

- We're a team, not individual officials. Be a good teammate. Don't throw your fellow officials under the bus. Never "bad-mouth" another official to anyone.

- Don't dwell on mistakes, no official has had a "perfect" game, learn from your mistakes and keep focused on each play.

- Read the Football Game Officials Manual to learn responsibilities and positioning for 4-man and 5-man; 3-man mechanics can be modified by the R.

PRE-GAME

- Have your bag packed and ready to go well before game time. (If you are transitioning from work to a game, you don't want to rush preparing your bag…you'll undoubtedly miss something.)

- Always have short sleeves and long sleeves in your bag…the weather can/will change quickly.

- Keep a copy of the rule book in your bag, but don't bring it to the field.

- Recommend you use a plastic container for flags, game cards, whistles, down markers, etc. It's much easier to keep track of everything.

- Always wear a proper uniform on the field. Don't dress on/near the field (i.e., don't wear running shoes to the field and then change to your black shoes).

- The uniform is your first "first impression." Keep your shoes clean/shined!

- Recommend you carry a backup whistle…one finger and one lanyard is a possible combination

- Arrive at the field when the R desires (in plenty of time to pregame with the entire crew)

- Ensure you understand your responsibility for KO's, counting, scrimmage plays, punts, FGA/trys, goal line, penalties.

- Communicate with the other wing to agree on hand signals

- Who has backward pass and motion responsibilities? (Going away or coming towards?)

- You'll step on the field 30 minutes before game time for varsity games, sub-varsity try to be on the field at least 15 minutes prior to KO.

- When the R speaks with the head coaches, you'll participate when he is speaking to your sideline's coach.

- Locate your ball boy/girl and record his/her name.

- (HL) locate your chain crew and record names.

CHAINS (WHAT TO TELL THE CHAIN CREW)

Note: try to get adults for the chain crew; don't be afraid to replace members of the chain crew if you don't feel they are appropriate. It's the home team's responsibility to provide adequate/capable members.

- No cell phone/walkman/I-Pod usage!

- You're an integral part of the crew...our job is to administer the game in a consistent rhythm. You can help us by hustling and paying attention.

- Have the crew ensure the accuracy (10 yards – set up from the 10 to the 20) and safety of the chains.

- Make sure there's a tape at the 5 yard mark of the chains.

- First priority is safety...drop the chains if the play is coming toward us.

- Always run through a few quick scenarios with the crew.

- Set up well off the field (two yards). This gives me plenty of room to work out-of-bounds.

- The Clip will be placed on the first available five yard line from the back stick...place the clip on the back edge of the stripe.

- Don't move until I wave you! (This is extremely important to emphasize.)

- When we mark off a penalty, box person do not move until I point at you (this reinforces the penalty enforcement spot and the penalty distance).

- After each play, box person can state the down (number) on the box and the line to gain (i.e., "I have three on the box, line to gain is the 42").

- If we have to measure, box person repositions to the front stick, keep the same down, then the stick people run onto the field as directed by the HL. Important that the down is not changed until after the measurement and the chains are re-set. HL needs to hold the clip and chain as you run onto the field to measure – if the clip falls off, you'll not get a very accurate measurement. If the clip is not on the five yard stripe nearest the rear stake, reposition it before coming onto the field for the measurement.

- Between first/second and third/fourth periods, HL will record, down, clip, line to gain. We will wait for the R to indicate we can move. We will then switch stick positions (the line to gain person should be the same after the switch), then hustle down to the other end of the field

- Do not snake your way thru the team box, or the members of the team and coaching staff near the sideline. Instead, move into the field, and around the team.

- Use the chain crew and ball person's names as much as possible… make them feel important as an integral member of the crew.

BALL PERSON

- The ball person will normally be younger than the chain crew. Sometimes (sub-varsity), the ball person will be a player.

- As with the chain crew, the ball person helps to administer the game in a consistent rhythm.

- If possible, the ball person should have two game balls.

- Use the ball person's name often; make him/her feel important.

- At all times (even when your sideline is on defense), the ball person should be right behind you (i.e., you are on the 15 yard line, the ball person should be right with you).

- If a pass is incomplete and away from another official, get a new ball and put that ball in play. Have the ball person chase the other ball.

- Note: If you are on a crew of 3 or 4 and the ball goes out of bounds or far away from you, officiate first, then get the ball...pause, clean up after the play, then get the ball (if at all possible have a player retrieve the ball).

A "TYPICAL" PLAY

- It will take time for you to become accustomed to the pre- and post-snap routines

- As a wing, you will count your sideline and confirm with another official who is counting the same players.

- Check for 7 on the line of scrimmage.

- Indicate outside receivers are OFF the Line of Scrimmage by "punching back". Keep this posture until the other wing acknowledges your signal. If the player then moves onto the LOS, indicate the change in position to the other wing.

- If you have 5 in the backfield, you only have 6 on the LOS (or you might have 12 players on the field)...indicate this to the other wing by tapping your flag, you'd like to have two flags with illegal formations.

Your keys: Snap, tackle, back

- Look for false starts

- At the snap, linemen will help you with the play…are they pass-blocking or run-blocking? What are the guards doing (pulling)?

Don't focus on the backfield…the referee has the backs at the start of the play. Look for linemen holding (on pass plays it's difficult to look for linemen holding while keying on the DBs and receivers - in this case, you will assist if possible on the tackle holding). When you move downfield on a passing play, your "internal clock" (about 3-4 seconds) will cause you to peek in the backfield to see what is going on with the play…but just a peek.

The referee will "hand off" the runner to you when the runner crosses the LOS. Allow the runner to go by you; on sweeps to your sideline, move towards the offensive backfield. This will prevent you from officiating from a "get out of the way "position. Still look for lead blocking problems (receivers on illegal blocks, pulling guards and lead blocking backs). Common fouls are Blocks Below the Waist – both offense and defense – and holding at the point of attack. Remember, if a player is gaining an advantage it may warrant a flag. Look for issues at the tackle (fumble, facemask, illegal helmet contact, sideline, horse collar, and other dead ball infractions.

When the play is dead by rule, you still have important responsibilities:

- If you are the covering official, sound your whistle, square off and indicate the ball's position with your "downfield" foot. Do not move until the ball is properly spotted. Unless the U or opposite wing has your spot, do not move to chase the ball…someone else can get it for you.

- Get off the sideline, move onto the field. Move to the numbers as you dead-ball officiate (watch players as they unpile and watch players away from the ball). This is known as "umbrella" – you'll do this on all most every play, try to keep all 22 players in front of you.

- Indicate the proper down with your hand and your voice (fist for fourth down)

- If the ball is dead and close to the goal line or line-to-gain, hustle in (sense of urgency) and get a forward progress spot. "Sell" the ball's position if needed. Review goal-line mechanics with your crew.

- If the play is going away from you, look for problems behind the play... clean up and be a good "dead ball" official.

- If the play ends out-of-bounds (OOB), whistle, signal TO, hold OOB spot with foot, keep your head up and continue to dead-ball officiate. Pivot your entire body to keep a good eye on players in the area (even substitutes).

- If the play ends up in the end zone, do the same thing...pivot your body and watch the runner/defenders as you give the "touchdown" signal.

- After a kick try, hustle to the middle of the field to clean up any shoving/taunting/etc. Use your voice to let the players know the play is over. Same on Field Goal attempts, but remember the ball may be still "live".

- "Sell" your calls if required (OOB on a catch, incomplete catch, player down before a fumble), but don't grandstand

BEAN BAG

- Bean bags are used to assist officials to mark a spot on the field (i.e. fumbles beyond the LOS, PSK enforcement spot, can be used to mark where a runner goes OOB, previous spots if box is not available)

- Carry two bean bags (in case you use one and the play moves well downfield)

- You don't need to throw the bean bag directly to the pile on a fumble or Post Scrimmage Kick (PSK) position. Drop it near your feet on the proper yard line

COMMUNICATING WITH OTHER OFFICIALS

- Kickoff: Raise your arm when you are ready for the kick. If another official is "up field" from you, wait until his arm is raised before you raise your own.

- Use the U to communicate with players, for example "#76 defense, is close to encroachment", don't say "#76 defense is encroaching" – coaches and players will wonder what other breaks are you giving their opponent. It's OK to communicate between plays, but make it quick and meaningful communication.

- Learn the proper football jargon and signals. When you throw a flag, continue to officiate until the ball is dead by rule. Then give a strong "tweet, tweet, tweet" to let the crew know you have a foul. Ensure you properly spot the ball and "clean up" before you report the foul to the R.

- When reporting fouls, ensure the proper forward progress spot is maintained.

- Report the foul slowly, and ensure your report has all the information that the R needs - for example: "live ball foul, holding offense #65, 10 yards from the spot of the foul, flag is in the correct spot". When marking forward progress, normally the wing closest to the dead ball will have the forward progress spot (although sometimes the closest official will not be able to see the ball). Both wing officials should agree on the forward progress spot.

- When you report the foul to the Referee, don't gesture or visually demonstrate what the player did. Just speak to the referee.

COMMUNICATING WITH COACHES

- Is the coach asking a question or making a statement? You don't need to answer if the coach is simply making a statement.

- Be "thick skinned"...do not be anxious to flag a coach...practice good conflict resolution.

- Be attentive to the coach's concerns, but maintain your focus on the game...do not delay the game to get clarification from another official.

- It's not about "us" as officials...understand and respect the coaching staff's time commitment and passion.

- Try not to run into coaches on sideline, communicate very clearly about your need for the first 2 yards on the sideline when the ball is live.

Possible statements for coaches:

- "Coach, what is your concern?"

- "Coach, what did you see?" (Ask the coach to clearly describe the foul.)

- "Coach, do you have a number?"

- "Thanks coach, I'll keep an eye on that"

- "My partner was right there and had a good look at the play"

- "If that's what happened, I missed it" (Just don't say that too many times)

- "Coach, I'm coming your way" (if he is in the restricted zone prior to the snap and you want to move him back)

- "Coach, I need you back please"

COMMUNICATING WITH PLAYERS

- When receivers come to the line, they will look to you to ensure they are properly lined up. Step onto the field if required to clearly communicate ("You're on the line" or "You're in the backfield"). Note: "You're on the line" and "You're off the line" sound too similar.

- At the sub-varsity level, you will encounter various levels of skill and knowledge so check with your R to determine how to approach the game; however, don't let "teaching" distract you from administering the game. At the sub-varsity level, you will see a lot of formation problems, false starts, etc. Communicate with your R if you have questions.

- Use your voice…("play's over!" if kids are jostling after the whistle).

FLAGS

- "Sky" the flag for dead ball fouls or fouls that will be enforced from previous or succeeding spot

- Toss the flag for a spot foul.

- If you throw the flag for a spot foul and don't like where it landed, move the flag (after you complete all other responsibilities) before you report the foul to the R.

- If you and the opposite wing throw flags, quickly come together and communicate to ensure you have the same foul…don't assume you have the same foul as the opposite wing, especially if multiple players move.

- If you throw the sole flag for a dead ball foul (i.e., false start), you can indicate the foul by quickly giving the proper signal…you don't have to run all the way to the R to report the foul.

PENALTY ENFORCEMENT

When you administer a penalty, each official has a role...typically:

- The LJ will "hold the spot" to indicate where penalty enforcement begins

- The HL after communication with the U will move to the spot where the ball will be marked ready for play (succeeding spot)

- Ensure you make eye/voice contact with the U to ensure proper administration

TIME OUTS (TO)

- When a coach or player requests a time out, loudly blow the whistle (tweet, tweet, tweet).

- First "look" should be to the clock to note the time.

- Then indicate the time out to the R.

- Officials usually indicate timeouts remaining by stating the number of the team that asked for the timeout first (i.e., "I have 23"...this means the team that just requested the time out has only two remaining and the other team has all three)

- After each TO, tell your coach how many TO's each team has left

AVOIDING AN INADVERTENT WHISTLE (IW)

- Do not blow your whistle unless you can see the ball!!! (We don't need a whistle on every play.)

- Are you the covering official? Typically, if the ball does not become dead in your side zone, you won't blow the whistle! There are some exceptions to this.

- Field goal attempt? Fair catch signal on a punt? Pile of players on a fumble? Don't blow your whistle to "protect" players during a fumble pile. If you don't see the ball - and most of the time you won't see the ball after a fumble - don't blow your whistle! (Be careful here, don't create an IW)

- In my opinion, a finger whistle wins out over a lanyard. A finger whistle gives you an extra fraction of a second to process what you see, and will often help you avoid an IW. (Note, most college and NFL officials use a lanyard whistle.)

- Take your time, don't be in a hurry to blow your whistle...(i.e., let a pass bounce twice)

Miscellaneous

- Always try to put the nose of the ball on a yard line to start an initial series for a team, (especially following a kick, fumble recovery by the defense, and interception)

- Before every snap, know exactly the location of the line to gain. LJ should be very vocal if the ball is downed close to the line to gain. HL, don't turn your head to look at the chains when the ball is downed. If you are unsure, look at the LJ for help.

- Be confident! If you are unsure about something (i.e., you think the crew has the wrong down or if you think a penalty is being incorrectly enforced), blow your whistle and speak with the R.

Appendix B
Dealing with Coaches and Sideline Control

The following was created by Randy Campbell to present to the Colorado Springs Football Officials Association in 2013.

Accept that by the very nature of the game, there will be numerous instances for the potential of volatile situations to surface. Your continual focus must be to communicate in all scenarios.

BEFORE THE GAME BEGINS

- Make an effort to get to "know" the coach (his personality, his overall demeanor, etc)

- You can ask another official who has had this coach before

- Establish a rapport before the game without causing concern with the opposing coaching staff

- Establish the same rapport with the other Head Coach - try to spend equal time

SPEAKING WITH COACHES
Never call coaches by their first names

Don't say too much too soon

- This is an IMPORTANT axiom to follow

- Ears cannot get you in trouble but your mouth can

- "Silence cannot be misquoted"

Be careful about using humor. It might help but be careful

Is the Coach asking a Question or Making a Comment?

- A comment does not require an answer unless it is a bad comment about you or the crew

- The person asking the question controls the conversation

- If you are not sure how to answer a question, make the coach repeat it

- If a coach asks for information, make every effort to get the CORRECT information to him as soon as possible

Be Respectful

- A coach wants to be assured that he has your attention

- Don't act distracted

- Use formal language ("By rule…")

- Keep communication brief

- Adopt a neutral tone and avoid personal remarks

- Stick to the issue at hand in a straightforward way

Let coaches have their say

- Adopt an instant "listening mode"

- Do not interrupt

Acknowledge the Coach

- "I hear what you're saying"

- "I understand"

- "I see what you mean"

GETTING THE HEAD COACH'S HELP

If there is a problem with players and/or team personnel being out of the team area or other situations, GO DIRECTLY TO THE HEAD COACH

BODY LANGUAGE

- Look the coach in the eye – do not stare but do make eye contact

- If a coach moves toward you to "get in your face," pivot sideways so you are shoulder-to-shoulder to him

- Be aware of body posture, facial expressions, head tilt and arm positions

- Don't use your hands when talking to a coach

- Don't touch a coach or player

IF YOU MAKE A MISTAKE...

- ...Admit it

- A simple apology is sufficient

- Do not elaborate or rationalize or make excuses

- "If that's what happened, we missed it"

IF THE COACH IS AGGRESSIVE

- NEVER meet emotion with emotion – take a deep breath

- When coaches raise their voice, lower yours

- Sooth rather than incite - try to diffuse a hostile situation by using your best people skills

- Make warnings deliberate and tactful

- The point of no return will be "DO YOU WANT TO REPEAT WHAT YOU SAID?" If he does, flag it

- Permit the coach to disengage. Nothing is gained by insisting on the last word

You and the Coach Differ
What do you do/say when the coach continues to complain about the same foul?

- "It had no effect on the outcome of the play"

- "We are not the penalty police"

- "Is this something you want us to call on both teams?"

Automatic Unsportsmanlike Foul by Coach or Player

- CHOKE SIGN and SIMILAR ACTIONS –

- Excessive and/or Vulgar Profanity that everyone can hear

- Use of ethnic slurs

After a Confrontation

- Recovery time

- How quickly do you recover when an adversarial situation or mistake has occurred?

Support Fellow Officials

- Never betray partners by showing that you doubt their judgment

- Indicate faith in your partner's decision

- "My partner had a good look"

- "What did you see from way over here"

PROMOTE SPORTSMANSHIP

Acknowledge a positive act by a player in front of his teammates and relay to the coach

SIDELINE CONTROL

- Use your "Get Back" coach

- "Coach, I need you back please"

- "Coach, I'm coming your way"

- When play comes into sidelines (especially bench area), look out of bounds and follow (visually) players into bench area

- One official at spot and one official covering fringe area

- When officials can touch one another, usually something is wrong

- Keep space between you

KEEP YOUR EGO UNDER CONTROL

- It's not about you!

- Remember, the reason we have officials is to make sure one team does not gain an advantage over the other team within the rules of the game

- Be a .300 hitter and not a .200 hitter

Appendix C
High School Athletic and Activity Associations

The following links will take you to your state's high school athletic and activity associations. Look for an 'Officials' page to find contact information for your local officiating association.

Alabama	http://www.ahsaa.com/
Alaska	http://asaa.org/
Arizona	http://aiaonline.org/
Arkansas	http://www.ahsaa.org/
California	http://www.cifstate.org/
Colorado	http://chsaanow.com/
Connecticut	http://www.casciac.org/
Delaware	http://www.doe.k12.de.us/diaa
Florida	http://www.fhsaa.org/
Georgia	http://www.ghsa.net/
Hawaii	http://www.sportshigh.com/
Idaho	http://www.idhsaa.org/
Illinois	http://www.ihsa.org/default.aspx
Indiana	http://www.ihsaa.org/
Iowa	http://www.iahsaa.org/
Kansas	http://www.kshsaa.org/
Kentucky	http://khsaa.org/
Louisiana	http://lhsaa.org/
Maine	http://www.mpa.cc/
Maryland	http://www.mpssaa.org/
Massachusetts	http://www.miaa.net/
Michigan	http://www.mhsaa.com/
Minnesota	http://www.mshsl.org/
Mississippi	http://www.misshsaa.com/
Missouri	http://www.mshsaa.org/
Montana	http://www.mhsa.org/

Nebraska	http://www.nsaahome.org/
Nevada	http://www.niaa.com/
New Hampshire	http://www.nhiaa.org/
New Jersey	http://www.njsiaa.org/
New Mexico	http://www.nmact.org/
New York	http://www.nysphsaa.org/
North Carolina	http://www.nchsaa.org/
North Dakota	http://www.ndhsaa.com/
Ohio	http://www.ohsaa.org/
Oklahoma	http://www.ossaa.com/
Oregon	http://www.osaa.org/
Pennsylvania	http://www.piaa.org/
Rhode Island	http://www.riil.org/
South Carolina	http://www.schsl.org/
South Dakota	http://www.sdhsaa.com/
Tennessee	http://tssaa.org/
Texas	http://www.uiltexas.org/football
Utah	http://www.uhsaa.org/
Vermont	http://www.vpaonline.org/domain/11
Virginia	http://www.vhsl.org/
Washington	http://www.wiaa.com/
West Virginia	http://www.wvssac.org/
Wisconsin	http://www.wiaawi.org/
Wyoming	http://www.whsaa.org/

Made in the USA
Columbia, SC
19 October 2022

69745038R00065